God's Rest Revealed

A Life Flowing With Milk and Honey

Antonio Palmer

God's Rest Revealed

Published by Kingdom Kaught Publishing, LLC.
Denton, Maryland U.S.A.

Printed in the U.S.A.

Cover design by Agape Advertisement, Inc.

Interior Design by Kingdom Kaught Publishing

Edited by Chad Steenerson, chad@jesusfreak.com

ISBN 978-0-9824550-0-5

Library of Congress Control Number: 2009905367

Dedication

I respectfully dedicate this book to the great people in my life who help me live what I'm preaching – my precious Lord Jesus Christ, my lovely wife Barbara, our radical-for-Jesus son Randy, my dear parents Lawrence and Carmenta, my sweet mother-in-law Deborah Ann, and bishop Donald Fulton and Pastor Becky Fulton.

Acknowledgments

There are so many friends who have helped me with this book. They listened to me hurl my "revelations" over and over again to them until I finally wrote them down. Some of them challenged me to finish the book (for Christ's sake), and others helped edit away my feeble grammar, realizing I was challenged in English class. Cheers to you all!

Special thanks to Bishop Larry Lee and Belinda Thomas, Pastors Leon and Via Crawford, Rev. Buford Harbin III, Pastors Charles and Darlene Carroll, Pastors Noland and Terri Henson, Pastors Frank and Stephanie Holloman, Pastor Jason Smith, Pastor David Whittington, Pastor Edward Ndumbu, Pastor Titus Kalyonge, Linwood and Roventa Smith, SFC Andria and Troy Gordon, Alleon Marquis Palmer, Danny Mazzeo, Xavier and Charlene Hawkins, Gwendolyn Blunt, and every son and daughter of The Ark, Inc.

Also, a special thanks to all the leaders, intercessors and prophetic people who prophesied this book "to come to pass."

Table of Contents

Introduction

"Wow! I didn't expect this response, but here they come," I said silently to the Lord. It was the oddest altar call appeal I've ever made. But the Lord knew what He was doing. And sure enough, as I gave the call, steadily they marched, filling up the altar as if they were assured that God was speaking directly to them. "If you've been sleepless or are suffering from insomnia, make your way to the altar. I want to pray the prayer of faith with you, and you shall be healed," I cried, "He wants to give you rest!"

The altar was filled to capacity. I couldn't believe all the people who were suffering from restlessness. There were myriad reasons why people were getting inadequate sleep or no sleep at all.

"I can't sleep because…":

- I lost my job and can't seem to find another one.
- I might lose my job.
- I'm stressed out.
- My house is going into foreclosure.
- Creditors keep harassing me.
- I'm going bankrupt.
- I have a lawsuit pending.
- I don't know if my husband loves me.
- My wife may be cheating on me.
- I'm worried about my child's future.
- I don't feel God will forgive me for what I've done.
- I keep seeing dark spirits in my room.
- I don't know why I can't sleep.

Insomnia is an inability to sleep, chronic sleeplessness[1]. Insomnia is a symptom of a sleeping disorder characterized by persistent difficulty falling asleep or staying asleep despite the opportunity[2]. Insomnia is defined as having difficulty falling asleep and/or staying asleep, which leads to a negative impact on the next day. It is a medical condition that touches the lives of approximately 60 million adults in the U.S. – making insomnia the most common sleep disorder[3]. Insomnia is not just physical. You can suffer from mental and spiritual restlessness as well. Neither Ambien, Lunesta, Restoril, lavender oil nor valerian root can heal spiritual insomnia!

The cure-all for this restlessness is found throughout history. The Israelites declared it in the Old Testament and the Jews still use it as a greeting today, *"Ma shlomcha?"* This literally means, "How is your *shalom?*" This question was once born out of a genuine concern for another but has been generalized and deduced to a mere greeting. My friend, "Ma shlomcha" is more than a mere salutation when passing by someone in the supermarket or on the street. Imagine in biblical times when a concerned parent would ask their child, "Ma shlomcha – how is your shalom?" It would put a demand on that child to give an account of their total life condition, just from the mentioning of the word "shalom" itself. Shalom means more than what we may think. Shalom means "wholeness (completeness), soundness, health, safety, wellness, prosperity, and peace." It carries the idea of *being well in every area of your life.* The question that I pose to you is, "Ma shlomcha – are you well in every area of your life? How is your shalom? Is there anything that is causing restlessness in your mind, body, soul or spirit?" If so, I encourage you to read through the pages of this book and discover the hidden treasure of God's Shalom. You will be able to give an account for your condition.

Shalom is God's rest for His people and it is revealed throughout the entire Bible:

> "Let the Lord be magnified, who has pleasure in the *prosperity* (shalom) of His servant." (Psalms 35:27)

> "For I know the thoughts that I think toward you, says the Lord, thoughts of *peace* (shalom) and not of

evil, to give you a future and a hope." (Jeremiah 29:11)

"For to be carnally minded is death, but to be spiritually minded is life and *peace*." (Romans 8:6 KJV – *"Eirene"* used here is the Greek equivalent of "shalom.")

"And the *peace* of God, which surpasses all understanding, will guard your hearts and minds through Christ Jesus." (Philippians 4:7)

"And let the *peace* of God rule in your hearts." (Colossians 3:15)

In 1 Thessalonians 5:23, the Lord is called "the God of *peace (eirene/shalom)."*

In all of his epistles to the church, the apostle Paul greets them with "grace to you and peace" (Romans 1:7; 1 Corinthians 1:3; 2 Corinthians 1:2; Galatians 1:3; Ephesians 1:2; Philippians 1:2; Colossians 1:2; 1 Thessalonians 1:1; 2 Thessalonians 1:2; 1 Timothy 1:2; 2 Timothy 1:2; Titus 1:4; Philemon 1:3). The apostle Peter also greeted the church in like manner (1 Peter 1:2 and 2 Peter 1:2). I believe the apostles realized that the shalom of God was a secret power to be experienced and practiced every day in the believer's life to sustain him for effective, righteous living.

During Jesus' earthly ministry, the people were burdened by the requirements of the Law and man-made rules that the Pharisees added to the Law which they could not uphold. I can imagine many of them being restless and having a great lack of sleep as they suffered from hopelessness and despair. This is why Jesus said, "Come to Me, all you who labor and are heavy laden, and I will give you *rest*. Take My yoke upon you and learn of Me, for I am gentle and lowly in heart, and you will find *rest* for your souls. For My yoke is easy and My burden is light." (Matthew 11:28-30)

Whether you cannot rest because of a racing mind, trying to solve problems, experiencing heartbreak, fearing demonic attacks, anxiety, financial insecurities or physical discomfort, Jesus desires to give you total rest, His *shalom*.

There are different types of rest:

- **Physical rest:** "And He said to them, 'Come away by yourselves to a secluded place and rest a while.' For there were many people coming and going, and they did not even have time to eat." (Mark 6:31)
- **Financial rest:** "Now if God so clothes the grass of the field, which today is, and tomorrow is thrown into the oven, will He not much more clothe you, O you of little faith? Therefore do not worry, saying, 'What shall we eat?' or 'What shall we drink?' or 'What shall we wear?' For after all these things the Gentiles seek. For your heavenly Father knows that you need all these things. But seek first the kingdom of God and His righteousness, and all these things shall be added to you." (Matthew 6:30-33)
- **Mental rest:** "And the peace of God, which surpasses all understanding, will guard your hearts and minds through Christ Jesus." (Philippians 4:7)
- **Emotional rest:** "Come to Me, all you who labor and are heavy laden, and I will give you rest…and you will find rest for your souls." (Matthew 11:28, 29)
- **Spiritual rest:** "The thief does not come except to steal, and to kill, and to destroy. I have come that they may have life, and that they may have it more abundantly." (John 10:10)
- **National rest** (rest from war): "The Lord gave them rest all around, according to all that He had sworn to their fathers. And not a man of all their enemies stood against them; the Lord delivered all their enemies into their hand." (Joshua 21:44)

- **Eternal rest:** "Therefore, since a promise remains of entering His rest, let us fear lest any of you seem to have come short of it." (Hebrews 4:1)

King David penned the most illustrated depiction of the Lord and His rest for us in Psalm 23:

> "The Lord is my shepherd; I shall not want. He makes me to lie down in green pastures; He leads me beside the still waters. He restores my soul; He leads me in the paths of righteousness For His name's sake. Yea, though I walk through the valley of the shadow of death, I will fear no evil; for You are with me; Your rod and Your staff, they comfort me. You prepare a table before me in the presence of my enemies; You anoint my head with oil; My cup runs over. Surely goodness and mercy shall follow me all the days of my life; and I will dwell in the house of the Lord forever."

> We are His people and the sheep of His pasture. (Psalms 100:3)

In this book, I will define and reveal God's rest, which is made available for you today. It is not just eternal, although that's the ultimate rest we seek to attain. However, you do not have to wait until you peel off this old body of clay to experience God's rest every day for the rest of your life. He promised it to you. It is a power that is made ready for us when we accept Jesus into our hearts. Why not receive it and activate it? This book will show you how to experience God's shalom, His rest – a *life* "flowing with milk and honey."

CHAPTER 1

God's Rest Promised

THE PROMISE

It was about 40 years into their wilderness experience when Moses declared to the Israelites, "Thou shalt remember the Lord thy God: for it is He that giveth thee power to get wealth, that He may establish his covenant which He sware unto thy fathers, as it is this day." (Deuteronomy 8:18, KJV) "That He may establish His covenant" is harmonious with the promise that God swore to Abram in Genesis 12:

> "Now the Lord had said unto Abram, 'Get thee out of thy country, and from thy kindred, and from thy father's house, unto a land that I will show thee: And I will make of thee a great nation, and I will bless thee, and make thy name great; and thou shalt be a blessing: And I will bless them that bless thee, and curse them him that curseth thee: and in thee shall all families of the earth be blessed.'" (Genesis 12:1-3, KJV)

Here we see the promise declared into the ears of Abram. At the age of 75, after many incantations to the fertility gods of his father Tehrah and paying daily homage to each little wooden idol set around his house, hoping that one day he could have a child born unto him, an audible voice pierced his faded hope with the promise of a lifetime: "I will make of thee a great nation." It was Abram's long-overdue dream! But the infinite God provoked Abram's finite thinking by basically telling him, "You're dreaming too small." I say this because, reading between the lines, He went above telling Abram that He'd give him a child. He tells him, rather, "I'll make you into a NATION." I can imagine Abram thinking to himself, "Let's see, do I want a child or a nation? I'll take the nation!" In addition, God states that not only will a nation arise from Abram, but his name will always be esteemed as the patriarch whose obedience gave rise to that nation. Moreover, God said, to everyone who blesses Abram, He will bless them; and to anyone who tries to curse Abram, God will curse them. But that's not all; God also promised that through Abram, every family on Earth who is descended from him shall be blessed. And by the way, God told Abram, "Since you're going to have such a great and large nation, they are going to need land. Let me show you the land I already picked out for them!"

Thus, Abram recapped, "Let me see; not just a child, but a nation with land, a great name, inextinguishable blessings, and every family who joins with me can be blessed because of what's in me. And all I have to do is leave my kinfolk and my country and go to the land which You already handpicked for me; deal or no deal? Deal! Pack up, Sarai, it's time to move!"

Did Abram think this was just his mind playing tricks on him? Perhaps, at first glance, like all other doubt that springs up after a great revelation from God. I know if I were Abraham, I probably would have been thinking, "After 75 years and trying everything else, this can't hurt me." So after shaking off the initial doubt, he obeyed the voice of God: "So Abram departed, as the Lord had spoken unto him." (Genesis 12:4)

LIVING PROOF

The Israelites didn't just believe in the promise of Abraham, they were living proof of that promise. They were part of the promise. They were the "great nation" part of the promise. Besides, if it had not been for Abraham's faith, they would not have existed at all. If

Abraham had not believed God, he would have remained at home talking to carved-out wooden images, possibly being influenced by demons, yet with no child; and if no child, then certainly no great nation. So the Israelites should have taken a good look at themselves and realized that they were the promise being lived out, even while they were in the wilderness. All they needed at this time was the land. Sometimes we, the spiritual Israel of God, the Body of Christ, need to take a good assessment of who we are today, and despite our greatest difficulty or "wilderness" experience, we need to realize that we, too, should not just believe in the promise but know that we are living proof of what God promised Abraham.

In Genesis 22:17-18, the Lord repeated the promise, "That in blessing I will bless thee, and in multiplying I will multiply thy seed as the stars of the heaven, and as the sand which is upon the sea shore; and thy seed shall possess the gate of his enemies."

From this passage of Scripture we can see that the "seed" or offspring of Abram was so numerous that we cannot comprehend how big the promise really was. This innumerable seed included the Israelites and those who are the seed of Abraham through faith in Jesus Christ. This is why we can look at ourselves and remind ourselves that we are living proof of God's promise no matter what obstacles we face.

HEAVENLY PLANNED

The remaining part of the promise for the Israelites in the wilderness was the possession of the land that God had promised. God knew that their possession of land would be a key component to their wealth. In biblical times, agriculture, farming, and produce were very significant sources of obtaining wealth. The Israelites were able to raise their livestock which fed on the land and grow their crops which yielded the large harvests throughout the year for commerce and trade, which resulted into Israel's wealth. Moses declared, "And you shall remember the Lord your God, for it is He who gives you power to *get wealth*" (Deuteronomy 8:18).

Possessing the promised land was a strategic plan from heaven. However, the Israelites could not possess the land without God giving them power to do so. Evidently, they either didn't have the ability to possess the land, or their ability was hidden from their mind's eye. God had to give them the power or ability. Without Him, they were unable to gain wealth or possess the land. *Getting* wealth isn't easy. The Israelites had to go through a wilderness experience to obtain it. Sound familiar? Little did they know that God was using the wilderness to deal with their inability to prosper. Their inability to prosper was because of their disobedience which God confronted in the wilderness. Their refusal to believe His promise held them back from receiving what God had in store for them. Disobedience will always cause us to be unable to prosper and bring to pass the things that God has promised us and longs for us to have.

GOD'S REST DEFINED

The land promised to Israel was called God's "rest." Rest was the buzzword amongst the camp's residents – physical rest from slavery and the hard labor of hauling heavy brick in the heat of the day to build houses and buildings that they would never own or be compensated for. They would find rest from their financial deprivation, from working without benefit or gain, from never having ownership of anything while being dependent upon the system of Egyptian rule for their meager provisions for daily survival. They needed rest from the mental anguish and oppression of their hard taskmasters. They needed rest from all the threats and reminders of their own inferiority. They needed rest from their men seeing their wives or daughters taken into Egyptian quarters to be violated and molested. Surely, the promised land would give them rest. The writer of Hebrews uses this term in addressing the New Testament Hebrew believers:

"Let us therefore fear, lest, a promise being left us of entering into His *rest*, any of you should seem to come short of it." (Hebrews 4:1 KJV – italics added)

In fact, in Hebrews 4, the writer actually used two different Greek words for "rest": *sabbatismos* and *katapausis*. Katapausis means "a calming of the winds." These winds can represent life's situations that may appear turbulent and cause great havoc. When a person has entered God's rest, these winds are calmed. The winds are tempered by activation of the authority of Christ in the believer. One example in the Gospels was when a storm came against the disciples' fishing boat as they were journeying across the Sea of Galilee to the country of the Gadarenes (Mark 4:35-41). As the disciples' lives were threatened by the storm and the raging wind, Jesus was resting. His rest was interrupted only by Peter's panic – Peter assumed that Jesus would dare to let them perish! Although traveling with Jesus' itinerant ministry was fascinating, Peter wasn't ready for his life to end, not even on a high note. Peter must have been thinking about all he had sacrificed to follow Jesus. Maybe he thought, "I left my family and occupation to become the first highly skilled fisherman killed on a boat – not today!" as he jarred Jesus awake from His rest. Awakened from His power nap, Jesus rebuked the stormy, emotional disciples and the stormy wind and said "Peace!" Then Jesus looked at the winds and the elements and commanded it to "be still." Jesus was living in the rest and peace of God while the disciples were succumbing to the pressures of their situation, i.e., the wind and the storm. The *authority* of Jesus overcame the elements and storms of humanity to bring calmness to Peter's perfect storm. We have this potent authority hidden within us. It is God's rest.

God's rest is contingent upon Christ's authority and our ability to exercise it in our lives. *Authority* (Greek *exousia*) means delegated power or the legal right to use power. Again, God says, "I give you power to get wealth." In other words, He was delegating to us His power or giving us legal right to exercise power to possess pros-

perity while living for Him. If God gives you the right to do something, then no demon from hell can take that right away or hinder
you from exercising it. You can calm financial winds, emotional
winds, marital winds, ministry winds, etc., with the delegated power
of God.

A RUSHING MIGHTY WIND

I'd like to encourage you by reminding you that you can calm any
wind because there is a stronger wind in you.

> "You shall receive *power* after that the Holy Ghost is
> come upon you…and when the day of Pentecost
> had fully come, they were all with one accord in one
> place. And suddenly there came a sound from
> heaven as of a *rushing mighty wind*, and it filled all the
> house where they were sitting…And they were
> filled with the Holy Ghost…" (Acts 1:8, 2:1-4 italics
> added).

This rushing mighty wind is the Holy Spirit. In John 3:8, the
Holy Spirit is likened to wind: "The wind blows where it wishes,
and you hear the sound of it, but cannot tell where it comes from
and where it goes. So is everyone who is born of the Spirit."

Have you ever wondered why the Holy Spirit is called "the Comforter"?

> "And I will pray the Father, and he shall give you
> another *Comforter*, that he may abide with you for
> ever." (John 14:16)

> "But the *Comforter*, which is the *Holy Ghost*, whom
> the Father will send in my name, he shall teach you
> all things, and bring all things to your remembrance,
> whatsoever I have said unto you." (John 14:26)

"But when the *Comforter* is come, whom I will send unto you from the Father, even the Spirit of truth, which proceedeth from the Father, he shall testify of me." (John 15:26)

"Nevertheless I tell you the truth; It is expedient for you that I go away: for if I go not away, the *Comforter* will not come unto you; but if I depart, I will send him unto you." (John 16:7)

The actual Greek word used in these above verses is *Parakletos*, which means "called to one's side," especially to one's aid. He, our Parakletos (Comforter), is a Helper who gives us divine strength we need to enable us to undergo trials and persecutions on behalf of the divine kingdom[4]. He is our Comforter because He has the ability to impart strength that overpowers every trial or persecution (stormy wind) that we'll ever face. The Comforter is simply one who comforts. To *comfort* means (1) to soothe in time of grief or fear: console; and (2) to make less severe or more bearable: relieve. "Comfort" is derived from the Latin intensive prefix *com*, and *fortis* meaning strong[5]. Thus, comfort originally mean "with or having strength." The Holy Spirit is called to our side to assist us with the kind of strength that soothes in time of grief, makes trials less severe, and more bearable. "God is faithful, who will not allow you to be tempted beyond what you are able, but with the temptation will also make the way of escape, that you may be able to *bear it*" (1 Corinthians 10:13). *Strength* is (1) power to withstand strain, force or stress; (2) power to sustain (keep from collapsing) or (3) resist (actively oppose) attacks. The Comforter is given to us to strengthen us (Ephesians 3:16), and to give us power to withstand any force against us and to help us actively resist attacks. The word strength (and its derivatives – strengthen(ed), strengtheneth, strong) is used 684 times throughout the Bible (Authorized Version, KJV). The Holy Spirit is called the Comforter because He has the important task of strengthening and re-strengthening our inner man with the ability to overcome life's storms. God's rest comes as an inner strength given by the power of the Holy Spirit.

The fresh wind of the Holy Spirit, the Comforter, will calm any tempestuous wind blowing against your life, for "Greater is He that is in you, than he that is in the world" (1 John 4:4 KJV). You have this power, this rushing mighty wind in you, and God wants you to activate it. It is this imparted, rushing mighty wind, the Holy Spirit, that causes you to be a witness, a revealed representative of Jesus, "And ye shall be *witnesses* unto me" (Acts 1:8 KJV, italics added). The witnesses of Jesus are given the Comforter to strengthen them and for the authority and legal right to calm every storm that you'll face. This is God's rest.

GOD'S REST IS HOLY

The other Greek word for rest is Sabbatismos, which means "a keeping of the *Shabbat (Sabbath)*." The Shabbat was the most important day for the Hebrew. Shabbat means "to cease and desist from labor, and rest." The Shabbat was commanded by God and held in light of God's resting from creation on the seventh day. To the Hebrew, it meant to stop creating and to enjoy the Creator and what has been already created for us. Sabbatismos was considered "holy" unto the Lord, and when it is not observed, it is considered unholy and disobedience to the commandment of the Lord.

Imagine God saying, "Take a break. If you don't, you're disobeying a direct order!" or "You will be disrespecting Me if you don't enjoy Me and what I've created for you."

If we are not careful, we can be carried away by our ambition to create a "good life" for ourselves, when in reality, through God, a "good life" has already been created for us. Everything God created, He declared it "good." God commands us to rest from the business of creating. We waste more precious time consuming our time of rest by trying to hammer out an ideal or comfortable lifestyle. We become workaholics at working on life. Then we find ourselves drained, depleted of energy, depressed, discouraged and feeling like

"What am I doing all this for?" Well, the Lord said, "Shabbat!" Cease from your own work and enter God's rest. Acknowledge the Lord, be thankful unto Him and bless His holy name. Be content with who you are and what He has already blessed you with. Enjoy who and what you have in front of you, even the trial. James said, "Count it all joy" (James 1:2). Paul said, "Rejoice always; and again I say rejoice. Be anxious for nothing" (Philippians 4:4, 6). "Godliness with contentment is great gain" (1 Timothy 6:6). Remember that "it is not by might nor by power, but by My Spirit, says the Lord of hosts" (Zechariah 4:6). This is holy unto the Lord.

Even in the wilderness, they were commanded to keep the Sabbath:

> "And remember that thou wast a servant in the land of Egypt, and that the Lord thy God brought thee out thence through a mighty hand and by a stretched out arm: therefore the Lord thy God commanded thee to *keep the Sabbath day.*" (Deuteronomy 5:15 KJV Italics mine)

The Sabbath was "holy unto the Lord." Rest is holiness. Please don't mistake rest for laziness. They are totally different. Rest is reflective, worshipful and celebrating, thriving on recovery from productive work, while laziness is idle and wasteful thinking and absorbs time with absolute nothingness. The Bible tells us to not be slothful (lazy), but to follow those who inherited the promises through their consistent walk of faith. (Hebrews 6:12) Laziness can never be categorized as holiness. God's rest, the Sabbatismos, is the kind of rest that restores and replenishes your mental strength and spiritual vitality so that you can be sensitive to revelation and wisdom that ultimately gives you insightful ability to attain wealth and resources that are flowing in the land for you, your seed and your ministry to the world as an ambassador of the kingdom of God. Going to conferences, seminars and retreats are wonderful. But such things should never take the place of your planned Sabbath. I'm not referring to weekly church services on Saturday or

15

Sunday. I'm speaking of scheduled (and sometimes urgent, un-scheduled), quality, unhindered and focused appointments of intimacy with God, reflecting on His goodness and tuning into His voice.

God's promise to Abraham was that he would be great and that his seed would be blessed and would inherit a wealthy land known as "God's rest." This place of rest symbolized the kind of life the believer could look forward to in Christ. It is receiving the steady comfort and strength of the Holy Spirit and living in legal, delegated operation of Christ's authority over life's storms. It is enjoying God the Father, Creator of life (and all things) and enjoying the life He has created for us and having cheerful expectation of the great things in store for your future. God promised that He would give Abraham's seed the power to get wealth (hidden in the possession of the land). Today, there is not only wealth hidden in the land, but a treasure hidden within us that can be released when we enter God's rest. God's rest supersedes material wealth (although it may include the abundance of possessions). God's rest gives you wealth (prosperity) in every dimension of your life. "Beloved, I pray that you may prosper in all things and be in health, just as your soul prospers" (3 John 2).

CHAPTER 2

Flowing With Milk and Honey

PROSPERITY IMPLIED

At least 19 times in the Old Testament, the land that God promised to give Abraham and his seed was described as a land *"flowing with milk and honey."* By using this description, God was implying prosperity. God first mentions this description while speaking to Moses at the burning bush about the deliverance of His people from their oppression. (Exodus 3:8) This is very significant because while God was planning their deliverance, He was also planning their "prosperity." His plan has not been altered. God still plans prosperity as well as deliverance for His people. In fact, not only does He plan it, He takes pleasure in it. "Let the Lord be magnified, who has pleasure in the prosperity of His servant." (Psalms 35:27)

According to the prophet Ezekiel, God personally searched out this particular land for His people and declared it to be the "glory of all lands." (Ezekiel 20:6, 15) God was giving His people the very best of the earth. We need to realize that God desires the best for His people, even today. Moses declared that it was a land "for which the Lord your God cares; the eyes of the Lord your God are always on it, from the beginning of the year until the very end of the year." (Deuteronomy 11:12) God eyed this land, cared for it (prepared it) for His people and waited for the right moment to allow them to possess it. The same is true with us. I believe that the Lord has eyed some land for us and has made preparation for us to possess it at the right moment in time. "Eye has not seen, nor ear heard, nor have entered into the heart of man the things which God has prepared for those who love Him." (1 Corinthians 2:9) He's prepared a land flowing with milk and honey, descriptive of the promise of entering into His rest. "Flowing with milk and honey" implied *a realm of sustained blessings, a cessation of lack.* This was considered rest.

GET WEALTH

The importance of possessing this land was that it translated into wealth. It meant economic empowerment! This was God's way of empowering His children to get wealth. (Deuteronomy 8:18) He promised it, prepared it for them, told them where it was and showed it to them, but it was left up to them to go get it. He promises it and prepares it, but we must go possess it.

He told Moses to send 12 men out to investigate the land. In other words, God was saying, "See it for yourself" or "I want you to see what I see." Consequently, when the 12 went out to spy the land, they came back with this report:

> "And they returned from searching of the land after forty days. And they went and came to Moses, and to Aaron, and to all the congregation of the children of Israel…and brought back word unto them…and showed them the fruit of the land. And they told him, and said, we came unto the land whither thou sentest us, and **SURELY** it *floweth with milk and honey*; and this is the fruit of it." (Numbers 13:25-27 KJV, emphasis added)

From all 12 spies' point of view, the land was SURELY flowing with milk and honey. They saw what God was seeing and what He promised. They even brought back clusters of grapes from the brook of Eshcol so that the rest of the people could see what they saw. These clusters were so enormous and heavy that it took at least two of them to carry the huge grapes on a staff (Numbers 13:23). Not only did they bring clusters of grapes but pomegranates and figs also. Deuteronomy 8:7-9 adds more details about the land:

> "For the Lord thy God bringeth thee into a good land, a land of brooks of water, of fountains and depths that spring out of valleys and hills; A land of wheat, and barley, and vines, and fig trees, and pomegranates; a land of oil olive, and honey; a land wherein thou shalt eat bread without scarceness, *thou shalt not lack any thing* in it..."

This Scripture passage includes the wheat and barley, vines and olive trees because of the significance of the grain, wine and oil that was also produced as rich commodities for children of God. The grain was so plentiful that they would never run out of bread to eat, the vines and grapes were in such abundance that wine would never cease coming out of the land, and a multitude of olives for the oils needed for ointments, perfumes, cooking, and most of all, the apothecary for anointing and consecration of continual ministry unto the Lord. It was a place of sustained blessings and cessation of lack! "Thou shalt not lack any thing in it!"

MILK AND HONEY

You may ask, "What is the relationship between the above-mentioned produce and the term 'milk and honey'?" Good question. Allow me to explain: We know that cattle, sheep and goats produce milk. In order for them to produce milk, they have to have plenty of fresh green pastures to graze in. For bees to give honey, they have to have plenty of flowers, fruits and vegetation to gather pollen from as they pollinate the plants. Because of green pastures and abundant produce, the livestock and the bees had no problem producing plenty of milk and honey. I speculate that the spies must have also observed that cattle, sheep and goats were plentiful and produced great quantities of milk in the abundant forage areas that they surveyed. During King Solomon's era, he sacrificed peace offerings of 22,000 oxen and 120,000 sheep. (1 Kings 8:63) On one particular occasion, when Solomon was dedicating the newly built Temple of the Lord, the Bible declares that he offered up so many sheep and oxen that they could not number them. There was an innumerable quantity of sheep, cattle and goats in the promised land, which translated into milk overflowing in abundance!

How did the land flow with honey? The honey came from various produce and plants, such as figs from the fig trees and dates from the date palms. Honey was also produced by bees from wild flowers and plants that were not cultivated in agricultural areas. These wild flowers and plants in the nonagricultural areas were known to blossom despite the adverse climatic conditions and were plentiful. So honey was supplied under any condition.

The Jewish Talmud (traditional writings) relates, "Our Sages saw goats eating from fig trees. The figs were so luscious that they were dripping with juice; the goats' udders were so full that milk simply flowed out. These two liquids mingled into a sweet stream creating a land that was literally "flowing with milk and honey." (Ketubot 111b)[6]

Thus, the description of a land "flowing with milk and honey" was an apparent description of great *abundance*. God was promising that He would supply His people with an *overflow* of resources that would never run out. "God will supply all your needs, according to His riches in glory through Christ Jesus." (Philippians 4:19) There is enough of God and His resources for all of us. Our cup can always "run over." The promise to enter into His "rest" is, by all means, an indication that we will enter into a life of abundance and prosperity.

It was evident from the testimony of all 12 spies that this promise was nigh unto them. With grapes in hand, they could literally taste the promise. The promise of prosperity was in their mouth! We have to get the promise of prosperity into our mouth and start speaking what God is speaking for our lives. However, there was still work to be done to take the Hebrews from seeing what God promised to the point where they could receive it.

THE NEVERTHELESS VIRUS

Have you ever wondered why prosperity is the leading controversial topic in the church today? It is because of what I call the Nevertheless Virus. This virus is a widespread pandemic sweeping across the Christian world and has penetrated every denominational line and seeks to devour the unity of the Body of Christ and its advancement. Let's take a closer look into this disease called Nevertheless.

> "NEVERTHELESS the people who dwell in the land are strong; the cities are fortified and very large; moreover we saw the descendants of Anak there. The Amalekites dwell in the land of the South; the Hittites, the Jebusites, and the Amorites dwell in the mountains; and the Canaanites dwell by the sea along the banks of the Jordan." Then Caleb quieted the people before Moses and said, "Let us go up at once and take posses-sion, for we are well able to overcome it." But the men who had gone up with him said, "We are not able to go up against the people, for they are stronger than we." And they gave the children of Israel a bad report of the land which they had spied out, saying, "The land through which we have gone as spies is a land that devours its inhabitants and all the people whom we saw in it are men of great stature. There we saw the giants (the descendants of Anak came from the giants); and we were like grasshoppers in our own sight, and so we were in their sight." (Numbers 13:28-33)

The Nevertheless Virus is the fear factor. It was the "what else" they saw besides the land flowing with milk and honey. They saw the Amalekites, Hittites, Jebusites, Amorites, Canaanites and most of all the GIANTS. Too often we get so fearful and intimidated by the strength of what else we see that we quickly forget that God has given us "power to get" whatever He promised us. The land and all of the resources in it were promised to them! God's power which He has given us is greater than the strength of giants. "Greater is He that is in us than he that is in the world" (1 John 4:4). Of course, we're not up against physical giants today; neither are we chasing after cattle, produce, and milk and honey. Instead, we are empowered to *get* money and resources. We will face satanic opposition attempting to hinder us from getting it. God has given you power to get "the money," honey. The Israelites could no longer say, "Show me the money!" God had clearly shown it to them. The problem now was in their getting ability. God gave them the power, but they had to do the getting.

The Nevertheless virus is a problem of cooperating with God. It holds us back from performing our part, the *getting*. The problem is actually a pursuing problem. Too often, I've had people come to me and say that they don't know how to get wealth (in any dimension). They always get stuck somewhere in the pursuit and give up because something intimidating changed their perception. The giants intimidated the Israelites' getting ability; then it became no longer worth the risk. They would internalize their external situations and view themselves as mere grasshoppers (Numbers 13:33). After this, they could no longer pursue the promise because their perception had been corrupted. Who told you about the giants in the first place? Why have you stopped pursuing what God has promised you? Who gave you an "evil report"? God said that the 10 spies who gave this addendum to the promise gave an evil report. It spread through the camp like wildfire. God then made another promise contingent upon their new-found belief; basically nobody in Moses' generation, except Caleb and Joshua, would obtain the promise because while the juice of the Promised Land's grapes was still in their mouths, they decided to worry about the same giants whom they took the grapes from. Little did they know that God was only using the strength of the giants to prepare the land for them while using His own strength to empower them to get the land! How often should we be reminded that the "wealth of the wicked is being stored up for the just." God is just utilizing the strength and skill of wicked men to prepare our wealth for us. We, on the other hand, just have to believe God and go get it!

POVERTY'S RELIGION

When Christians stop pursuing wealth, they can become very religious in their view about money. The perspective of some in the church is that we shouldn't have much money. This causes great controversy, because while they are trying to be pious with nothing, there are others who are pursuing the promises of every aspect of God's rest, including prosperity, so that they can be a blessing to the world. This religious viewpoint is not new. It has been around for centuries. It is called asceticism.

Asceticism is defined as "a way of thinking that sees money and things as evil." To the ascetic, the less you own, the more spiritual you can be. If something isn't essential, you shouldn't have it. This is a "poverty is piety" belief system. I call it "poverty's religion." While their intentions are right, that is, to live holy lives, their doctrine is totally wrong.

Poverty is defined as "the state of having little or no money and few or no material possessions."[7] If poverty is piety, then why would the patriarch Job say it is oppression? When Satan went to tempt Job, he asked God if he could take all of Job's "stuff" from him. If having abundance is wrong and poverty can help you to be more pious, wouldn't Satan rather desire for Job to keep all his stuff than to strip him down to nothing? If poverty was piety, then Satan helped Job to live right by taking all his stuff! I'm pretty sure that Satan's intentions were quite different. I'm convinced that by reducing Job to poverty, Satan wanted Job to backslide and curse God. Furthermore, why would God reward Job at the end of his major trial with twice as much as he had before if prosperity was wrong?

Asceticism is a symptom of the Nevertheless Virus. Ascetics are so fearful that wealth will cause them to be unholy that they grow so accustomed to the "wilderness experience," convincing themselves that struggling financially until the afterlife is simply part of the will of God for themselves and for others. They indoctrinate others into this belief and ultimately cause controversy in the Body of Christ.

THE ASCETIC'S EXCUSE

The ascetic's justification for having a lack of money is that money or wealth will make a person materialistic. After all, God did forewarn Israel that they would perish if they were to forget Him, serve other gods and act in the same manner as the other occupants of the land. God indeed forewarned them not to forget Him; however, He didn't say "Forget about getting the wealth that I promised you, because I'm afraid you're going to forget me." If that was the case, I don't think He would have ever made the promise. Ascetics thrive on the idea that they have power over their wilderness experience. They have the strength to endure their never-ending financial struggles. It is their testimony. However, the wilderness was intended to be seasonal, not last a lifetime. In fact, the wilderness is the place that prepares us for the promised land, not the place that keeps us from it. It is not a permanent place, but a temporary one. It is not your permanent duty station; it is only boot camp! Allow me to exhort you to stop making your residence in the wilderness. Stop being persuaded by the evil report of those who master poverty to look powerful. God is making you healthy enough to get wealth and handle it. Poverty is not God's rest! If you can be strong in the wilderness, you can be strong in Canaan. If you can be victorious in poverty, you can be victorious in prosperity.

PROSPERITY IS NOT MATERIALISM

Prosperity and materialism are two different things. Let me differentiate between the two:

Prosperity is defined as the condition of being prosperous, successful or thriving economically[8]. It is simply the obtaining of abundance, especially but not limited to material goods. The apostle John puts another twist on the word "prosperity" in 3 John 2 when he says, "I wish above all things that you would prosper and be in health even as your soul prospers." (KJV) The Greek word used in this Scripture verse is *euodoo*, which means "to have a good or *safe* journey." To the Christian, this implies that as we walk this course of life as pilgrims in this world, we will abide in God's will and His truth, and we will enjoy His blessings. If material abundance causes us to be unsafe in our Christian walk, then we should stop seeking it until we are strong enough to handle it. However, Scripture does imply that as our soul prospers (journeys safely), God desires that we prosper materially or have financial safety (security). As mentioned in the introduction, prosperity is a dimension of God's shalom and He takes pleasure in you having it. (Psalms 35:27)

Webster's New Collegiate Dictionary defines materialism as "a theory that physical matter is the only or fundamental reality and that all being and processes and phenomena can be explained as manifestations or results of matter." Two other definitions flow from the first: "A doctrine that the only or the highest value or objectives lie in material well-being and in the furtherance of material progress," and "*preoccupation with or stress upon material* rather than intellectual or spiritual things."[9]

Many people confuse prosperity with materialism simply because we assume that you have to have a lot of material possessions or money in order to be considered materialistic. This is far from the truth. There are people in every financial class who are materialistic. That's right, even the poor can be materialistic. If a poor person lusts to have money and pursue after it with selfish motives and for selfish gain, he is materialistic whether he obtains an abundance of material wealth or not.

The Bible often uses words like greed, filthy lucre, lust and covetousness to express materialism. These are attitudes and are developed through a belief or way of thinking. The apostle Paul describes this attitude or belief system in 1 Timothy 6:5, where he warns Timothy that some men would teach that "gain (abundance) is godliness." Neither abundance nor the lack of it makes you godly. Your lifestyle with or without abundance is what determines godliness. It is your attitude toward money and what you do with it in the sight of God that brings merit to your godliness. He goes on to say, "For the *love of money* is the root of all evil." (1 Timothy 6:10, emphasis added) If you have an unhealthy craving for money and material things that causes you to do manipulative deeds, then you are materialistic and need to be delivered.

Materialism carries the idea that having money gives you some type of favorable status in the world, and for some people, even with God. The world has the notion that money can buy anything, but we know that it cannot buy right standing with God. The monetary value for a right standing with God was Jesus' redeeming blood! And He alone paid for our righteousness in full! Having money can allow you to buy things that give you temporary happiness, but the joy of the Lord is priceless. As a matter of fact, those who are constantly chasing after money, especially for the wrong reasons, even the poor, fall into temptations and snares and end up "piercing themselves with many sorrows." (1 Timothy 6:9-10) Jesus said, "What is a man profited, if he shall gain the whole world and lose his own soul?" (Matthew 16:26) Remember, in the pursuit of the promise, keep your soul. We should always remain as God-chasers while pursuing His promises. His promise is a promise of rest. Material wealth is just one aspect of this multidimensional promise.

Contrasting materialism and prosperity is simple. Prosperity is simply having abundant resources. Materialism is having the wrong concept about and doing the wrong things with the abundance of resources that you possess. If materialism is labeled as prosperity, then I will call it "wicked prosperity" or the "wealth of the wicked or unrighteous." This is why the Lord told David, "Fret not thyself because of him who prospereth in his way, because of the man who bringeth wicked devices to pass." (Psalms 37:7 KJV) Throughout the book of Proverbs, you find the contrast between wicked prosperity and righteous prosperity. Men like Job, Abraham, Joseph, Boaz and David all were wealthy, but righteous.

Materialism and asceticism are beliefs, attitudes and actions centered around money (or the lack of it) that are completely wrong. It is not prosperity that is wrong in and of itself. You can be prosperous, even materially, and live right. While I agree that having material abundance brings a wealth of responsibility and plenty of temptations, it is not the money that will destroy the man, but his craving and unhealthy attachment to it, or his wrong belief about it.

It is my belief that God desires abundance for His people, that is, the ones who allow Him to prepare them to handle the responsibilities and temptations that come with it. He is looking for a holy nation, a royal priesthood, a peculiar people that will believe Him for a land flowing with milk and honey.

A CALEB SPIRIT

While the 10 spies were infecting the camp with the Nevertheless Virus, Caleb attempted to calm and reassure the people that they could and should take pursuit of and possess the land. He was confident that they could overcome every obstacle, including the giants. Do you think Caleb was too materialistic? I don't think so. In fact, God commended him (and Joshua) for their tenacity of pursuing after the promise. He promised them that because they kept the right perspective and did not feed into the negativity of the other spies, they were going to inherit the promise.

We need a Caleb spirit in the church today, having the ability to go after the things of God the right way. The name Caleb means "capable or able." Caleb says, "We are well able to overcome it." (Numbers 13:30) We need people of God who are going to stand up and reassure the church that we are *overcomers*, not just spiritually but financially as well. We need to say to ourselves that we are "well able" to overcome every obstacle and possess our promise of prosperity and peace. Why are we well able? We are well able because the Lord has made us "more than *conquerors* through Him who loves us." (Romans 8:37) "For whatever is born of God overcomes the world. And this is the victory that *overcomes* the world – our faith." (1 John 5:4) "Greater is he that is in us than he that is in the world." (1 John 4:4) Shake off the grasshopper mentality about who you are in God and know that you can defeat any-thing, even the spirits of poverty, selfishness and greed. Like Caleb, you can possess the promise of prosperity with a clean heart. There is still a rest that belongs to the people of God if we are willing to face the giants.

In Numbers 14:8, Caleb and Joshua pleaded with the congregation (approximately 2 million people) that "if the Lord *delights* in us, then He will bring us into this land and give it to us, a land which flows with milk and honey." To Caleb and Joshua, the Lord's "delight (His pleasure and favor)" was revealed in His bringing them to the land in order to give it to them. They further likened refusal to enter the land and fearing the people of the land as rebellion against God: "Only *do not rebel* against the Lord, *nor fear* the people of the land, for they are our bread." (Numbers 14:9, italics mine)

The Lord would reward Caleb and Joshua by allowing them to enter the promised land while an entire generation would fall short of it. The reason why God allowed Caleb entrance was because he had a "different spirit in him and has followed Me fully" (Numbers 14:24, Joshua 14:8, 9).

To have a Caleb spirit is to have a different spirit, a spirit that will believe the promises of God and not accept the negative report and rebellion of others and to fully, wholeheartedly follow the Lord. A Caleb spirit is needed in order to enter God's rest. A Caleb spirit is needed in order to quiet life's storms. Paul reminds us, "God has not given us a spirit of fear, but of power, and of love, and of a sound mind" (2 Timothy 1:7). That's a Caleb spirit – no fear, but love, power and sound-mindedness. Neither has God given us an ascetic doctrine, a negative promise or a weak, impoverished mindset, but rather an obedient spirit of getting, conquering and blessing the world by demonstrating His love through sharing the resources that God enables us to obtain.

CHAPTER 3

An Open Heaven

In the previous chapter, we disclosed the Old Testament's view of God's rest as a land flowing with milk and honey. This God-given analogy described the innumerable livestock providing an overflow of milk and the plants and bees that produced a steady flow of honey. The milk was produced by the livestock that ate from a great supply of green pastures, and the honey was produced from the multitudes of fruits and plants. We must understand that the land could only be fruitful and abundant in green pastures if it had a sufficient supply of water; without water, there wouldn't be any milk and honey flowing. A sufficient supply of water was the key to it all. God's rest operated upon His release of the waters from above. God had to open the floodgates of heaven and frequently pour out a blessing, i.e., the waters (Malachi 3:10), in order for the land to flow with milk and honey.

Water is used quite frequently throughout the Bible in symbolic fashion, typically representing the Holy Spirit and the Word of God. Living in the supernatural realm of God's rest requires a sufficient supply of the Word of God and fellowship of the Holy Spirit. I earlier explained God's rest as it pertained to the Holy Spirit, the Comforter. Now I will explain the importance of the Word of God in connection with God's rest.

GETTING THE WATER

In Moses' comparison of Canaan (the promised land/God's rest) with Egypt, water is used with both positive and negative connotations. Moses contrasts the distinct difference between the two lands and their agricultural development, showing the significance of water, particularly rain for Israel:

> "For the land, whither ye go to possess it, is not as the land of Egypt, from whence ye came out, where thou sowedst thy seed, and wateredst it with thy foot, as a garden of herbs: But the land, whither ye go to possess it, is a land of hills and valleys, and drinketh water of the *rain of heaven*." (Deuteronomy 11:10-11 KJV, italics mine)

Enslaved in Egypt, the Israelites underwent the strain of cultivating the land by collecting wheelbarrows full of water from the Nile River to water the seeds that were sown, only to end up creating a means of wealth (abundant crops) for the Egyptians. At the end of the day, they were exhausted and depleted of strength, probably in desperate need of more than your average foot massage. They "wateredst it (the land) with thy foot" (Deuteronomy 11:10). In Biblical symbolism, *water* represented wisdom, *Egypt* symbolized "the world," and *abundant crops* symbolized prosperity and wealth. Having the Israelite slaves draw water from the Nile River by foot, in order to water the land for a bountiful harvest was Egypt's way of doing things, i.e. their wisdom. It was hard, toiling work independent of biblical instructions. Any wisdom independent of sound, biblical instructions is considered *worldly* wisdom or the wisdom of men. Make no mistake; it produced bountiful crops for the Egyptians. It is through worldly wisdom that unregenerate men gain their wealth or prosperity. Worldly people can have material success independent of God. But there is a distinct difference between the material gain of worldly people and the material gain of godly people. Worldly wealth is called the wealth of the wicked because the wicked do not glorify God or propagate the Gospel of Jesus with it and some utilize it to fulfill their evil lust or spread it to promote ungodly agendas such as pornography, abortions, sex slave trade, etc. The wealth of the righteous is used for righteous living and for advancing the kingdom of God on Earth.

OPEN HEAVEN

In Canaan (the promised land/God's rest), the water supply was not going to come from the established rivers, or by the foot of men, but from the rain of heaven. Israel was not going to obtain wealth, prosperity or abundance the same way the Egyptians did. God does not want His people to obtain wealth through worldly wisdom. In Canaan, He would send the water supply directly from heaven (Deuteronomy 11:11). He was going to open the floodgates of heaven and send the rain! And the Body of Christ cannot exist in the supernatural realm of God's rest without rain from heaven.

When it rained in Israel, it was indicative of an *open heaven*. We often use the phrase "open heaven" as a spiritual metaphor for miracles, healings, deliverance and the power of God. This idea of supernatural blessings being poured out from an open heaven is a spiritual likeness compared to natural rain coming down from heaven, which was sent by God to produce a great harvest. The natural rain watered the land and produced a harvest which for the Israelites meant wealth, prosperity and abundance for the Children of Israel. This *rain* was supplied by God. It wasn't something that they could get "by foot" like the Egyptians. God had to release it! Without God opening the floodgates of heaven, the land could not produce its crops. The nation would experience unrest. Without an open heaven, there is no rest. Rain assured rest. Spiritually, the "rain of heaven" represents the source of wisdom that is revealed to godly people for their success both spiritually and materially. It is *rhema*, the revealed Word of God. Our source of wisdom is totally different from the wisdom of this world. Our wisdom proceeds from the mouth of God:

> "For as the *rain* and the snow come down from
> heaven, And do not return there without watering

the earth, And making it bear and sprout, And furnishing seed to the sower and bread to the eater; so will *My word* be which goes forth from My mouth; It will not return to Me empty, Without accomplishing what I desire, And without succeeding in the matter for which I sent it." (Isaiah 55:10, 11)

God's word is like the rain that comes down from heaven. Its purpose is to water the earth and make it bring forth and bud, that it may provide seed for sowing and bread for eating. The bread is for our provision; the seed is for our prosperity. The bread is for our necessity; the seed is for our ongoing opportunity to bless others. As long as we continue to sow the seeds and the heavens remain open, the ground has to yield a harvest of more bread and seed. It becomes a continual cycle that the Bible calls "seedtime and harvest." It is the law of reciprocity that is eternally established. We must take caution, however, that we do not eat our seed and waste our bread. Too often this is the case with many Christians. We do not sow back into the kingdom. Instead of sowing, some rather purchase the latest fashionable clothes or eat at fancy restaurants with the monies that should have been tithed or sown into the kingdom. This is an example of eating seed and wasting bread. Anyway, the rain is intended to bring bread to eat, but seed to sow.

THE RAIN ACCOMPLISHES

According to Isaiah, the rain will accomplish God's desire and succeed in His intended purpose for sending it. (Isaiah 55:11) The rain is sent from heaven to accomplish God's desire and purpose. Thus, spiritually speaking, the rain, which is the Word of God, causes us to live to accomplish God's desire. That's living in God's rest! That's how we live a life flowing with milk and honey!

Isaiah poetically illustrates the effect and accomplishment of the rain:

"For you will *go out with joy* and be *led forth with peace*;
the mountains and the hills will break forth into
shouts of joy before you, and all the trees of the
field will clap their hands. Instead of the thorn bush
the cypress will come up, and instead of the nettle *the
myrtle will come up*, and it will be a memorial to the
LORD, for an everlasting sign which will not be cut
off." (Isaiah 55:12,-13 NASB, italics added).

When the rain comes and starts fulfilling God's desire in us, we
"go out with joy and are led forth with peace (shalom)." Without
the rain, we go in one way – unfruitful, joyless and discouraged; but
with the rain, we are led out in joy and peace (soundness, wellness,
prosperity, health, safety). The rain, the Word of God, empowers us
to live well in every area of our lives – Shalom. The apostle Paul
said, "The kingdom of God is…righteousness, joy and peace in the
Holy Spirit." (Romans 14:17) When the heavens are open and the
rain descends, we begin to experience the supernatural realm of
God's rest.

The rain will replace the thorns and briers and produce *cypress*
(fir) and *myrtle* trees and it will bring perpetual honor (a memorial) to
His name. (Isaiah 55:13) Thorns and briers (nettle) are indicative of
uncultivated land or wastelands. Thorns and briers are marks of an
unfruitful, barren life usually symbolic of wicked men. (2 Samuel
23:6, Isaiah 27:4, Micah 7:4)[10] Barrenness was always paralleled with
a cursed life; however, the rain is sent out to replace this barrenness
or cursed life with the cypress and myrtle trees.

The cypress or fir (Hebrew *berosh*) tree was used for several
things such as musical instruments, doors for houses, ceilings, decks
of ships, flooring and spear shafts.[11] The *fir* tree and the *myrtle* are
emblems of the godly to which the saints are sometimes compared
(Zechariah 1:10), because they are good to look at, of a sweet smell,
ever green, flourish in watery places and bring forth fruit.[12] Because
of its variety of uses, the fir tree can further signify godly men
bringing forth fruit from their ability to minister to a variety of
needs.

The *myrtle* tree was a lowly evergreen shrub that had a beautiful fragrance, producing the most exquisite perfumes. The Hebrew word for myrtle is *hedes*, from which comes *Hadassah*, the original name of Esther. We know that Hadassah was a beautiful young virgin called into the kingdom, in God's perfect timing, for the divine purpose of delivering the Jewish nation from total destruction. Thus, the myrtle tree represents a person whom God raises up for the distinct purpose of delivering His people from destruction.

The rain, which is the Word of God, is sent out to transform our wicked, unfruitful lives that are doomed for destruction and make us into godly people with special abilities to minister to a variety of needs and to help deliver people from destruction. This is what the rain will accomplish. This is what Jesus accomplished on the cross. God sent His Word and made it flesh. I must remind you that He had a crown of thorns thrust with merciless cruelty upon His head before He was crucified. The crown of thorns was indicative of our barren, cursed lives that He took to the cross in exchange for a more prosperous and blessed life that we can now live. So from Isaiah 55:12-13, we can conclude that the promised land was just a shadowy portrait of the life God so lovingly desires for us to live, a *life* flowing with milk and honey.

DRINK THE RAIN

Even though there may be an open heaven, abundance is still predicated upon how we *drink* the rain.

> "For the earth which DRINKS IN THE RAIN that often comes upon it, and bears herbs useful for those by whom it is cultivated, receives blessing from God; but if it bears thorns and briers, it is rejected and near to being cursed, whose end is to be burned." (Hebrews 6:7-8, emphasis mine)

The earth (land) must "drink" the rain from heaven in order for it to yield abundant crops. If the earth is too hard and has not been broken, tilled or aerated, it will tend to not "drink" the rain and therefore not produce crops. Any farmer will tell you that fallow ground must be broken first before it can produce healthy crops. (Jeremiah 4:3; Hosea 10:12) In order for us to have God's rest, we must be "broken." *Brokenness* is essential to peace and godly prosperity. Brokenness is the condition of being crushed by intense pain or grief. Have you ever experienced grief in your life to the point that you didn't know which way to turn? Was it so overwhelming that you just felt like throwing in the towel? Ironically, this is where God likes to begin His plan to prosper you, both spiritually and materially. He knows this is the posture of life that can help us drink in the rain.

To illustrate brokenness, King David writes, "The sacrifices of God are a broken spirit, a broken and a contrite heart – these, O God, You will not despise" (Psalms 51:17) and "The Lord is near to those who have a broken heart, and saves such as have a contrite spirit." (Psalms 34:18) David goes on to say that our hearts become broken by "many afflictions." (Psalms 34:19) These afflictions or troubles are intended to get our hearts to a place of dependence upon God, demonstrated by our crying out to Him. (Psalms 34:17) Jesus said, "I have told you these things, so that in me you may have peace. In this world you will have trouble. But take heart! I have overcome the world." (John 16:33, NIV) The phrase "told you these things" is indicative of the rain, the Word of God that Jesus declared to His disciples. His Word (rain) was for them to have peace (shalom). Jesus knew they would face troubles. The troubles would break them to the point of crying out to Him as they recognized that He alone has overcome the troubles of the world. Thus, in King David's life, God is able to "deliver him (the righteous) out of them (afflictions/troubles) all." (Psalms 34:19)

Whenever a potter is making a new vessel from an old one, he first breaks the old one to start the process of reshaping it and making it into what he desires it to be. The Lord is our potter and we are merely clay in His hand. (Jeremiah 18:1-7) He has to *break* us in order to reshape us into a vessel that can handle the life He desires for us.

The fallow ground of our hearts is broken so that we can drink the rain. The word *"drink,"* as defined by Webster's Collegiate Dictionary, means "to soak up" or "to take in avidly through the senses or intellect." When the land drinks the rain, it must soak it up. To soak up something means to absorb it, to be immersed in it, to allow something to deeply permeate, flow or spread throughout. The land must absorb the rain and allow it to flow and spread throughout it in order for it to produce abundant crops. Again, if the rain is symbolic of the living Word of God or revelation, then the earth (land) which drinks in the rain in Hebrews 6:7 is symbolic of us, God's people. Thus, God's rest, the land flowing with milk and honey, involves the heart and mind of God's people and our ability to "drink" His Word. We are that land that must drink the rain. Our hearts and minds must *soak up revelation* from the Word of God and let it spread throughout all our senses and intellect so that we can produce an abundant life. The heavens can be open, but if we don't drink, we won't experience shalom – God's rest. We must drink the rain in order to remove our "thorn and brier" condition and become like the fir and myrtle trees. If we drink of the heavenly rain from God, we can have a life flowing with milk and honey.

THE LAND

Whatever the land yields when the rain falls upon it determines its condition. It will either bring forth herbs (crops), or it will produce *thorns and briers.* (Hebrews 6:8) If it brings forth crops, then it is good ground conditioned to drink the rain. If it brings forth thorns and briers, it's an indication that the ground is still fallow and so hardened that it refuses the rain.

The condition of the land is contingent upon the cultivation process, i.e., "by whom it is cultivated (dressed)." (Hebrews 6:7) The dresser or farmer is responsible for preparing the land so that it may drink. In this spiritual sense, I personally see farmers as pastors whom God has divinely appointed over our souls. They are gifts from God which He has enabled to mature the saints and strengthen the Body of Christ for the work of the ministry. (Ephesians 4:11-12) The pastor can prepare us to drink the rain so that we can become like those fir and myrtle trees. I am convinced that we can live a much more productive and prosperous life if we simply allow these genuine pastors to cultivate us. We must surrender to the cultivating work of the pastor. (Hebrews 13:17) The good ground is those whose lives have been broken to the point of total dependence upon God and who have yielded to the cultivating work of their pastor.

When the land bears thorns and briers, it is "rejected and near to being cursed." Again, the thorns and briers are a product of a lack of cultivation. A lack of cultivation does not mean that there was no one there making an effort to improve the land. It simply means that the land had no desire to improve. It is sad to say that there are some "Christians" who do not allow their pastor to cultivate them for improvement in their life. Either they think they can do it on their own or they see the pastor as merely another human anointed just to share a sweet sermon on Sunday. Indications of people who may not receive cultivation are those who don't attend Bible study, cell groups, morning worship or even sow financially into the ministry and vision of the local assembly. Their lives are still the same as they were 3, 5 or 10 years earlier. There are some who attend church services regularly but who are troublemakers, backbiters and faultfinders. These are those who never allow the Word to soak into their hearts. Hosea 4:6 says, "My people are destroyed for the lack of knowledge: because thou hast rejected knowledge, I shall also reject thee." God rejects those who reject His knowledge. This is experiential knowledge, not mere information; not a sweet sermon, but a life-developing word from the Lord. If we don't drink the rain, we will ultimately be rejected, cursed and burned.

But if we, the land, drink of the rain from heaven, we will produce healthy crops. Notice how the crops (herbs) are "useful for those by whom it is cultivated"? I want to suggest two Biblical points here: First, the crops could mean good conduct and godly character made evident to the pastor as a sign that someone is drinking (taking in) the Word of God and yielding to the pastor's cultivation. Second, the crops can mean material resources that you have gained from receiving the wisdom of God and are sufficiently yielding them to the pastor to help with the ministry of the local church. These crops are useful for the pastor to utilize for ministry and to further the work of the Kingdom. Both of these points will receive blessings from God.

God opens the heavens to pour out His rain of revelation and wisdom, and He expects His people to bear fruit, both spiritual and material, which in turn enable them to deliver many people from destruction and fulfill a variety of needs. These are the people who will receive blessings from God. "Be fruitful and multiply!"

There is a great transformation taking place. Jesus has come to take away our thorn-like condition and replace it with a fruitful condition. When He died on the cross, He took our curse away. Now we are without excuse to be transformed into blessed people. Jesus is taking us from bondage and delivering us into prosperity. He snatched us out of bondage with the hope that we would believe that He will lead us into an abundant life. Jesus said, "The thief cometh not but to steal, and to kill, and to destroy: I am come that they might have life, and that they might have it more abundantly" (John 10:10). This abundant life is a balance of both spiritual and material wealth for the work of the ministry, to glorify God and to honor His name perpetually. This abundant life comes as we are conformed to His image and transformed with a renewed mind. This abundant life is a "*life* flowing with milk and honey." It is God's rest revealed.

CHAPTER 4

Thank God for Your Wilderness

Many Christians go through life without ever experiencing the realm of God's rest – a *life* flowing with milk and honey. How often they are stuck in the wilderness and never come close to the open-heaven experience. The wilderness is an essential process that every child of God must face before experiencing a life flowing with milk and honey. As stated in an earlier chapter, some people become so accustomed to their wilderness experience that they mistakenly accept it to be a normal way of life. God never intended for us to stay in the wilderness phase. It is a transitional phase that we must face before entering God's rest or living the abundant life.

THE WILDERNESS DEFINED

As we define the word *"wilderness,"* we understand it to mean "a *barren*, uninhabited region left in its natural condition, usually a wildly grown forest area or a sandy, dry desert accompanied by the perils of wild beast." Notice that the root of the word "wilderness" is "wild." Something that is wild is something that lacks discipline, restraint or control. Thus, the wilderness is a place where things are out of control, or I'd like to say, out of *our* control. We actually refer to it as a "trial, test, or trouble." God surrounds us with wild things to get the wildness out of us. It is common to see wild beasts in the wilderness. The Bible often refers to people who are known to be *trouble*makers and evil as *wild* beasts. These people, along with troubling situations, can create a life-threatening environment for us, thus, our wilderness experience. The wilderness is the trial of life, the trying of our faith that is so out of control and out of our control to the point that it appears severely perilous to us. It threatens our mind, our marriage, our finances, our ministry, our children, our faith, our attitudes and even our lives. Ironically, we need the threats of the wilderness in order to advance to the place of abundant living.

THE PURPOSE OF THE WILDERNESS

"And thou shalt remember all the way which the LORD thy God led thee these forty years in the wilderness, to humble thee, and to prove thee, to know what was in thine heart, whether thou would-est keep his commandments, or no. And he humbled thee, and suffered thee to hunger, and fed thee with manna, which thou knewest not, neither did thy fathers know; that he might make thee know that man doth not live by bread only, but by every word that proceedeth out of the mouth of the LORD doth man live." (Deuteronomy 8:2-3, KJV)

Don't be disappointed and apprehensive because of this revelation that God has a purpose for the wilderness. His purpose is revealed here in Deuteronomy 8:2-3, where Moses says that God uses situations "to humble thee and to prove thee, to know what was in thine heart, whether thou wouldest keep his commandments, or no…that he might make thee know that man doth not live by bread alone, but by every word that proceeded out of the mouth of the Lord doth man live." There are four reasons why God takes us through the wilderness:

1. To humble us
2. To prove us
3. To know what is in our hearts, whether we will keep His commandments or not; and

4. To make us know that man does not live by bread only, but by every word that proceeds out of His mouth.

TO HUMBLE US (HUMILITY)

The first purpose of the wilderness is to *humble* us. According to Webster's Dictionary, to be humbled means to be made lower in condition or status, or to be humiliated. Humiliation is when your pride has been knocked down or abased. You have been reduced to a lower position in your own eyes as well as in the eyes of others. It also carries the idea of mortifying, which means to subject to severe embarrassment or to destroy the strength of something. *Humility* is a derivative of humiliation. You cannot become humble until you have been humiliated or severely embarrassed. The wilderness should "destroy your strength" to the point of needing to depend upon another.

There is no pride killer like embarrassment. The wilderness experience was an embarrassment to the Israelites. While they were looking for immediate occupation of the promised land, God had them undergo severe, life-threatening situations that became the byword and derision of other nations. Dry, scorching heat with no food and sometimes no water, no weapons of warfare and the constant threats of wild beasts, venomous snakes and scorpions were the prevailing circumstances surrounding the daily life of the Hebrew nation. How long could anyone live in these conditions? Although they had escaped the Egyptian army, they could not evade the sweltering heat of the desert. The Egyptians mocked them for leaving Egypt only to end up in a deserted death box. The Bible says that it was the "reproach of Egypt." (Joshua 5:9) As long as the Israelites stayed in the wilderness, the Egyptians had something to laugh about. This was embarrassing to the Israelites. I can hear the mocking: "Where is this God that you claimed was taking you into a land flowing with milk and honey?"

No matter how much you learn to endure in your wilderness experience, it is still embarrassing to be in that condition for too long. You can smile, walk upright and even praise God like never before, but it still leaves the stench of humiliation as you are terminally stuck in the middle of your dry season. No matter how we mask it or master it, the wilderness is still an unpleasant position to be in.

The wilderness will make you or break you. People who do not humble themselves will never see the oasis that God has placed in the wilderness. As a result, they may murmur and complain, constantly bringing to light their discontent and dissatisfaction with God. How ungrateful the Israelites were, failing to consider the amazing provision of God despite their arrogant requests. God performed miracle after miracle to reassure them of his provision and protection. He made bitter waters turn sweet, provided fresh manna from heaven each morning, gave them an overstock of quail (until it "ran out of their nostrils)," and most of all, He had a special place (the tabernacle) custom-built for His residence among His people. He did this so that they would know that He was always there with them, that they were not alone in this wilderness experience. But they failed to hold onto these signs, rather opting to continue in their constant, foolish complaining. Sometimes when we are going through extreme circumstances, we are inclined to forget God's presence in the time of trouble, His provision and His protection. When we start listening to the voices mocking our faith and our advancement, we will view the wilderness irritatingly, as an embarrassing misfortune or disaster instead of something advantageous and for our good. We would fail to realize that this is the route to the promises of God, His rest – a life flowing with milk and honey. Instead of murmuring and complaining, we should give God thanks for the wilderness.

What embarrasses you? What is the thing that you feel you can't get out of or away from that others know about, ridicule and shake their heads in disgust? Is it a marriage that is broken, a defiant child, an overwhelming financial debt, a rollercoaster ministry that never seems to grow or a business going bankrupt? What is your reproach, your shame? Why is it a reproach? Why are you so ashamed of your wilderness experience? I have the answer: It appears as failure to the world and to you. Pride makes us see our failures as failures. When we humble ourselves, we begin to see things from a different perspective. As we begin to depend upon God, we start seeing things as He sees them. Our failures become stepping stones to success and our wilderness becomes an opportunity for God to grow us, lead us and build us a lasting life of honor and greatness. It is not God's mission to embarrass you, but to empower you. He is thinking about your success, your future and your prosperity. As stated in chapter 2, when God was planning your deliverance, He was also planning your prosperity. He knows the plans that He has for us. (Jeremiah 29:11) The wilderness is just part of the process pushing you toward the fulfillment of God's ultimate plan for your life. The wilderness is part of God's plan to empower you to succeed. He has to humble you through the wilderness process. "*Humble yourself* under the mighty hand of God and He will exalt you in due season." (1 Peter 5:6, italics added)

SUBMISSION

"God resists the proud, but gives grace to the *humble*. Therefore *submit* to God. Resist the devil and he will flee from you. Draw near to God and He will draw near to you." (James 4:6-8 italics added)

This passage of Scripture reveals a key component of humility, which is submission. To *submit* means to *willingly surrender or yield oneself to the will or authority of another.* Understanding authority is the key to submission. There is no real humility without an authority to submit to. Authority is the right to use power or to establish and enforce rule. You will have a big problem with obtaining the promises of God if you cannot submit to authority. Many people are stuck in the wilderness and may ultimately die there because they don't submit to authority. Notice that I did not say tolerate authority. I said submit to authority. Submission must be done willingly, not grudgingly. So many church folk are just tolerating or "putting up with" their pastor. If he asks them to do something, they do it grudgingly or ask several questions before they end up doing a halfhearted job. That's not submission; that's just toleration. A real person of humility knows that they do all things "as unto the Lord." God counts submission to His messenger, i.e., your pastor, as though you were literally submitting to Him. Mark the person who follows instructions thoroughly. That's the person who is rich toward God and is in position for the promise. It is Joshua and Caleb anticipating an assignment from Moses. Joshua could hardly wait to follow commands from Moses as he camped at the edge of the mountain, waiting for Moses to share what God had spoken to Him on the mountaintop. Are you confident that your pastor has your God-given destiny hidden in his mouth? Do you respect him (or her) as the prophet leading you to a "life flowing with milking and honey"? "Submitting yourself unto God" often requires your submission to the authority of His servant to whom He has delegated the right to govern your life. "Believe in the Lord your God, and you shall be established; believe His *prophets* (your pastor), and you shall prosper." (2 Chronicles 20:20, emphasis added)

RESIST THE DEVIL

In order to resist the devil, we must first submit ourselves unto God. What you resist directly relates to whose authority you are submitting. Allow me to explain: If you are submitting to God's authority, you cannot resist Him. You cannot resist and submit to an authority at the same time. To *resist* means "to *actively* oppose or to fight with force." Therefore, if you submit yourself to someone, you cannot at the same time fight against them. If you are fighting their authority, then naturally you are not submitting to their authority. Fighting against an authority is *rebellion*. You cannot yield and rebel simultaneously. There must be an authority in direct opposition to what you have yielded to. So, to paraphrase, God says, "Submit to my authority and then fight forcefully against the devil; rebel against him and he will flee." You can only cause an uprising, a rebellion, a revolution against the devil and overthrow his systems after you have submitted to the authority of God.

The wilderness is a place of training of learning which authority to submit to and which authority to resist. Everyone who rebelled against God's authority died in the wilderness. The reason for your desert experience is to kill your disobedience. God desires your submission to Him. It is the key to your entering into God's rest, possessing and maintaining a life flowing with milk and honey. If you submit to God and resist the devil, the devil will flee from you. He will flee from your mind, your family, your finances and your ministry. The devil only flees from a person who forcefully fights against him and who submits to God. Take aggressive action against the devil and he will dodge out of sight (at least for a season).

God wants you to depend on Him. There are things in your wilderness that He already knows are too difficult for you to conquer on your own. In Psalm 91, Moses gives a list of such things: the snare of the fowler, the noisome pestilence, the lion and the adder, and arrows taking flight at night. God knows we need Him. And if we submit to God, none of these things shall harm us. He designed it that way. "He who dwells in the secret place of the Most High shall abide under the shadow of the Almighty. I will say of the Lord, He is my refuge and my fortress; my God, in Him I will trust." (Psalms 91:1-2) It was He who led us in the wilderness, and only He knows how to lead us through the wilderness and completely out of it. There are no situations in your life that are too uncontrollable or violent for God. If you depend on and yield to Him, He will direct your path out of the most undesirable, life-threatening situations and cause your enemies to scatter. Moses' submission to and trust in the Lord was so great he said, "**SURELY** He shall deliver (us) ..." (Psalms 91:3).

THE DEVIL'S PHOTOGRAPH

The archenemy of humility is *pride*. While humility is the hallmark characteristic of the Son of God, Satan's most noticeable characteristic is pride. Even Satan knows that a proud look is an abomination, a detestable thing in the sight of God. When God sees pride, it's like a constant reminder of Lucifer's failed insurrection in the kingdom of heaven (Isaiah 14:12-15). Having the look of pride on our faces is like scheduling a personal photograph of the devil himself.

In James 4:6, it is evident that God is disgusted with pride so much to the point of resisting, i.e., actively opposing people. Humility causes us to resist the devil, but pride causes God to resist us. *Pride is the attitude of living independently of the life of God.* Pride is a destructive force. Nations have fallen because of pride. Kingdoms have been divided because of pride. Marriages fail when pride rules dialogue and deed. Pride never lets you forgive or repent. Pride goes before (precedes) destruction and a haughty spirit before a fall. (Proverbs 16:18) Whenever you see something ruined or destroyed, you don't have to be a crime scene investigator to know that pride had something to do with its downfall. Pride sets the stage for failure. It's even the cause of shame. (Proverbs 11:12) Genuine leaders prosper through humility. But many have fallen in their prosperity because they failed to remain humble. Pride kills ministries, darken hearts and leaves family members in petty disputes long after the funeral of their deceased loved one. You cannot live a life flowing with milk and honey if you're choosing to live a life independent of God. Pride keeps you from God's rest, making you feel shameful, unfulfilled and insecure. Surely proud people can have money, but they will never find God's rest. Something will always be terribly wrong with their lives no matter how much material wealth they obtain, because although they have money, it is hard for pride and peace to reside in the same place. And God's rest is a place of peace – Shalom.

TO PROVE US

The second purpose for the wilderness is to "prove" us. The Hebrew word used in Deuteronomy 8:2 for prove is *nacah*, meaning "to test, to try, to tempt, or to put to the proof of." Abraham went through a nacah episode with God at Mount Moriah when he was instructed to kill his only son, Isaac. (Genesis 22) There are other Hebrew words synonymous with nacah, including *bachan, kazab* and *qadash,* which all carry the same meaning of trying or testing. The life of Job is also a great example of God "proving" His people. Job declares, "He knows the way that I take; when He has tested (proved) me, I shall come forth as gold." (Job 23:10) I cannot think of anyone else who has had a more severe testing than Job. He lost all of his children, most of his servants (except the ones who reported to him all the bad news), his property was set on fire, his livestock (finances) was killed and his health deteriorated rapidly. All this happened in a matter of days. To add to his dilemma, his wife tried to influence him to "curse God" and his friends thought that he must have committed some terrible sin or was rebelling in some way against the Lord and that he was being repaid for his evil. But in all this, Job kept the faith and came out as pure as gold! Job figured out that what he was experiencing was the "trying of his faith." Peter called it the "fiery trial" (1 Peter 4:12) and told us to not think of it as some strange or bizarre thing.

Job likened himself to gold being put to the test. The prophet Malachi parallels this analogy by giving us a metaphoric depiction of the purifying process of gold. "Who may abide the day of His coming? And who shall stand when He appeareth? For He is like a refiner's fire and like fuller's soap. He will sit as a refiner and a purifier of silver; He will purify the sons of Levi, and *purge them as gold* and silver, that they may offer to the Lord an offering in righteousness." (Malachi 3:2-3 KJV, emphasis added)

Malachi says that God will *purge them as gold* (and silver) and rid them of their impurities. This is exactly what Job felt when going through his trial. He was being "purged by the Refiner."

THE REFINING PROCESS

Some fascinating facts about gold are that it is the most stable of all metals. It will never lose its quality. You will never be stuck with an inferior product. Gold is gold. Gold is also the most malleable of all metals, capable of being shaped by the beating of a hammer. Gold can be hammered into sheets less than 5-millionths of an inch thick. It is also the most ductile (capable of being drawn out very thin). A single ounce of gold can be drawn into a wire 35 miles long (and an ounce of gold in coin form would be only about as large as a half dollar!). Gold is indestructible and imperishable. It is a very stable and durable metal. Gold will not evaporate, mildew, rust, crumble, break or rot. It can always be recycled. Gold can stand indefinite immersion in salt water (consider what salt water does to glass!), it does not tarnish in air and it can resist almost any acid. The articles of gold discovered from ancient times (such as in Egypt) are as perfect as when they were first made several thousand years ago![13] Job saw himself like gold! If we are to endure fiery trials, we must see ourselves as gold. We must know that we:

- Are the most consistent
- Will never lose our quality
- Are not inferior to any other
- Can be shaped and take the beating of the hammer and are stable and durable
- Will never crumble or break under pressure

The refiner, sometimes called a goldsmith or smelter, crushes the gold to the size of lentils and then grinds it to powder in a handmill made of granite slabs. This powder is then spread upon a slightly inclined stone table and water is poured over it to wash away the earthly materials. The comparatively heavy gold particles are gathered from the table, dried and melted in a closed crucible with lead, salt and bran, and kept in a molten condition for five days, at the end of which time the gold comes out pure.[14]

Looking at the refining process, we can see that God, who is our Refiner, allows us to go through crushing, grinding, washings and melting in order to purify and shape us into His image, i.e., a peculiar people.

This is all done to rid us of all the contamination of other "metals" and "debris" until we are in our pure form. The fire of the Lord melts away those things that attach themselves to our true nature, which is the image of God. It takes the Refiner's fire to bring to the surface this true nature. The more we allow Him to refine us, the closer we find ourselves to the brink of the Jordan River, ready to enter the realm of God's rest.

THE VALUE OF INSTRUCTIONS

The third purpose for the wilderness is for God to see whether or not we will keep His commandments. Two interesting words are found in this statement: "keep" and "commandments." The Hebrew word for *keep* is *shamar*, meaning "to observe, guard, or give heed to." The Hebrew word for *commandment* is *mitzvah*, meaning "precept, principle, law, or instruction." The commandments of the Lord are not just to be followed, but safeguarded in the heart. Whenever a person has something of great value such as jewelry, wills, title deeds and other important documents, they are normally secured in a safe or a bank vault. Similarly, if the commandments of the Lord are of great value and importance to you, then your heart must become like a bank vault to safely store and secure these valuable instructions from any intruder or thief. It is the objective of the enemy of our soul to steal these away from us. "The thief does not come except to steal, and to kill, and to destroy." (John 10:10a)

These life instructions and principles are greater in value than any earthly possession. They are to be "shamar*ed*," or given heed to. When you follow thoroughly the instructions of the Lord, you will unlock the secret of blessings "overtaking" you. (Deuteronomy 28:1) Attached to every instruction is a blessing, and the only way to obtain it is to thoroughly obey the given instruction. God's rest is hidden in the tapestry of His divine commandments. In fact, the Lord told Joshua to meditate upon the commandments day and night and that he would ultimately be a man who would make his way prosperous and of good success. (Joshua 1:8) You cannot live a life flowing with milk and honey without deeming the instructions of God as the most valuable commodity there is. "Poverty and shame shall be to him that *refuseth instruction*: but he that regardeth *reproof (instruction)* shall be honoured." (Proverbs 13:18 KJV, emphasis mine)

MILK, HONEY AND SPIRITUAL BREAD

The final purpose of the wilderness is "Man shall not live by bread only, but by every word that proceeds out of the mouth of the Lord." Bread, in this passage of Scripture, implies food of any kind. The significance is placed upon the fact that in order to exist naturally, we need food. You cannot continue to be physically sustained if you go too many days without food. Likewise, for anyone to live spiritually, they must rely on "every word proceeding out of the mouth of the Lord."

Jesus, while being tempted in the wilderness, used this same Scriptural truth to extinguish Satan's fiery attempts to get Him to turn stones into bread (food). Even after 40 days without eating any food, Jesus still knew not to abort His Spirit-led fasting assignment. He knew that the Holy Spirit led Him into the wilderness to be tempted of the devil. He could've easily agreed with the devil and miraculously turned the stones into bread. After all, He was indeed in need of food, but because it was a suggestion from the enemy, even though he was using Scripture, it was an obvious choice to refuse to agree with him.

Jesus, when quoting "every word proceeding out of the mouth of the Lord," was not just warding off the enemy with any passage of Scripture, but a rightly divided word. It was the relevant word for His "right now" situation.

A pastor friend of mine, Bishop Joseph Norfleet, once gave an analogy of the meaning of "a word proceeding out of the mouth." He mentioned the Genesis 22 story about Abraham being instructed by God to offer up his son Isaac as a sacrificial offering on Mount Mariah. This initial instruction became a word proceeding out of the mouth of God. No matter how illogical it seemed to Abraham, it came from the mouth of God, and Abraham set out to obey Him. However, at the moment that Abraham had Isaac pinned to the altar with his knife lifted in a ready-to-strike position, God sent another instruction by way of the angel of the Lord. The angel of the Lord instructed Abraham, "Do not lay your hand on the lad, or do anything to him; for now I know that you fear God, since you have not withheld your son, your only son, from Me." (Genesis 22:12) When the angel of the Lord came with this "new" instruction, it became the word "proceeding out of the mouth of the Lord" and the old instruction became a "preceding word" which had to be voided by Abraham. Had Abraham missed the new instruction and stayed with the old proceeding word (which became the "preceding" word), he could have killed Isaac and reaped the consequences of his inability to hear God.

I believe that we circle the wilderness because we sometimes have a serious problem hearing God for a "word proceeding out of His mouth." We get stuck on the "preceding word." I often call this "stale bread" or "molded bread." The wilderness is our training ground to make us sensitive and ready for fresh bread proceeding out of the mouth of the Lord. Living in God's rest is contingent upon having a trained ear that hears God's word proceeding from His mouth.

CHAPTER 5

The Stench of Disobedience

Many Christians fail to realize the importance of the wilderness experience. It is an umbilical cord to the promised land and can only be cut away through a life of obedience. God's rest, a life flowing with milk and honey, is developed only through the trying of our faith. Oftentimes, we try to evade or lighten the load of our suffering, only leaving scars of unfulfilled promises and underdeveloped character. This is exactly what happened to the wilderness wanderers. Their evasion of character development led to a strong stench of dead carcasses decaying in the heat of the desert.

UNBELIEF

I believe one of the best passages of Scripture that explains why the original Exodus generation did not enter God's rest is Hebrews 3:7-19:

> "Therefore, as the Holy Spirit says: 'Today, if you will hear His voice, do not harden your hearts as in the rebellion, in the day of trial in the wilderness, where your fathers tested Me, tried Me, and saw My works forty years. Therefore I was angry with that generation, and said, 'they always go astray in their heart, and they have not known My ways.' So I swore in My wrath, 'they shall not enter My rest.' Beware, brethren, lest there be in any of you an evil heart of unbelief in departing from the living God;

but exhort one another daily, while it is called 'To-day,' lest any of you be hardened through the deceitfulness of sin. For we have become partakers of Christ if we hold the beginning of our confidence steadfast to the end, while it is said: 'Today if you will hear His voice, do not harden your hearts as in the rebellion.' For who, having heard, rebelled? Indeed, was it not with those who sinned, whose corpses fell in the wilderness? And to whom did He swear that they would not enter His rest, but to those who did not obey? So we see that they could not enter in because of unbelief."

In verse 19, the author of Hebrews uses the Greek word *apistia* for *unbelief*. Apistia means unfaithfulness, weakness of faith, failure to demonstrate faith, faithlessness. The Israelites did not enter into God's rest because of their apistia, their *failure to demonstrate faith*, or because of their faithlessness. Several attributes of apistia (unbelief) are given in Hebrews 3:7-19. The Israelites:

(1) **Hardened their hearts:** The word for hardened is *skleruno*, which means to become obstinate or stubborn, to be harsh, rough, violent, offensive and intolerable. Because of their stubbornness, the Israelites did not make it into the promised land.

(2) **Tested and tried God:** They *peirazo* and *dokimazo* God. Peirazo means to tempt by exhibiting distrust as to prove whether (God) is not justly distrusted. In other words, they challenged God and justified their challenge by citing that they had a reason to distrust Him. They were looking for any excuse as to why they didn't believe Him. Dokimazo carries the meaning of seeing whether something is genuine or not, like the testing of metal. They tried God negatively by seeing whether He was genuine.

(3) **Always went astray in their hearts:** They *aei planao*, always, perpetually, at any and every time were led into error, fell away from the truth.

(4) **Did not know His ways:** They did not *ginosko hodos*, which means they did not become acquainted with His course of conduct, His manner of thinking, feeling, and deciding. They wanted the benefits of God without God.

(5) **Departed from the living God with an evil heart of unbelief:** Because of their hearts siding toward wickedness, they departed, *aphistemi*, became standoffish and withdrew themselves from the living God. It was a voluntary withdrawal.

(6) **Heard but rebelled:** They heard the instructions and promises, yet they rebelled, *parapikraino*, which means they resisted God's authority to the point of arousing His indignation. They irritated God and produced a bitter taste in His stomach. This is what parapikraino means. They made God sick!

(7) **Sinned:** They *hamartano*, which means they violated God's law, trespassed, missed the mark, wandered from the path of honor. When the prodigal son (Luke 15) "came to himself," he said, "I will arise and go to my father, and I will say to him, 'father, I have sinned (hamartano) against heaven and before you, and I am no longer worthy (I dishonored myself) to be called your son...'" He wandered from the path of honor! He was at the point of eating carob pods out of the swine pen. He disgraced himself.

(8) **And did not obey:** They *apeitheo*, which means they did not allow themselves to be persuaded. They were very obstinate and non-compliant to the divine will of God. They were firm in their resistance to change.

Recapping, we see that the wilderness wanderers were harsh, intolerable, offensive, exhibited distrust, challenged the genuineness of God's character, erred in their hearts on any and every occasion, didn't try to become familiar with the way God does things, became standoffish and voluntarily withdrew themselves from God, resisted His authority, dishonored themselves, did not allow themselves to be persuaded and were adamant in their refusal to change and submit to the divine will of God. Wow! Do you know any "believers" like this? The apostle Paul referred to similar "unbelieving believers" in 2 Timothy 3. Can we expect to enter God's rest with this type of faithlessness?

The apostle Paul informs us that these things were written for our example (1 Corinthians 10:11) and that we should be diligent to enter God's rest, lest any one of us fall according to the same example of unbelief (disobedience) (Hebrews 4:11).

DISOBEDIENT DESPITE THE MIGHTY MAN OF GOD

The one thing that perplexes me the most about the whole wilderness story is that the Israelites had one of the most dynamic leaders of all time – Moses. Yet, they still rebelled against God. In my opinion, besides Jesus Himself, Moses stands second to none in leadership and power. God dealt with Him as a friend and proclaimed Him the meekest man who ever lived. After discovering who he really was, an Israelite, Moses refused to enjoy the pleasures of the Egyptian palace and chose rather to suffer hardship with the people of God. He endured 40 years of training in the desert before becoming the mighty deliverer that he was. God used him mightily with signs and wonders in Egypt and in the wilderness. He was the pastor of an entire nation (approximately 2 million people). Yet, the people whom he sacrificed his life for rebelled against him and God. No wonder God was angry! I believe that a life flowing with milk and honey is a life that also displays great honor for the person whom God has ordained to shepherd you. We must learn how to receive and honor the messenger as well as the message.

THE DANGER OF DISOBEDIENCE

Disobedience ultimately causes God to become angry. He is the last person you want angry at you. God became so angry at the disobedient Israelites that He began to "swear." "So I swore in My wrath, 'They shall not enter My rest.'" (Hebrews 3:11 (also Psalms 95:11))

The word "*swore* (swear)" in this Scripture verse is the Greek *omnuo*. This word means "to affirm, promise, or threaten with an oath." In this case, God threatened or promised the Israelites that they would not enter into the promised land and He did it with an "oath." What is an oath? The Greek word *horkos* is translated "oath," meaning a vocal affirmation of the truth of one's statement generally made by appealing to a deity. It is taken from the Greek word *herkos*, meaning a boundary, fence or limitation. The oath limits the declarer by the binding of a curse or punishment. The curse or punishment is the strength of the oath. It usually settles the issue because the "gods" have heard the declaration and now have the right to punish the declarer if they do not follow through with their promise. The declarer is now bound by his word and cannot take it back.

A prime illustration of the declaring of an oath is found in Matthew 14:1-11:

> "At that time Herod the tetrarch heard of the fame of Jesus, And said unto his servants, This is John the Baptist; he is risen from the dead; and therefore mighty works do shew forth themselves in him. For Herod had laid hold on John, and bound him, and put him in prison for Herodias' sake, his brother Philip's wife. For John said unto him, It is not lawful for thee to have her. And when he would have put him to death, he feared the multitude, because they counted him as a prophet. But when Herod's birthday was kept, the daughter of Herodias danced before them, and pleased Herod. Whereupon *he promised with an oath* to give her whatsoever she

would ask. And she, being before instructed of her mother, said, 'Give me here John the Baptist's head in a charger.' And the king was sorry: nevertheless *for the oath's sake,* and them which sat with him at meat, he commanded it to be given her. And he sent, and beheaded John in the prison. And his head was brought in a charger, and given to the damsel: and she brought it to her mother."

Salome, the daughter of Herodias, who was the wife of Herod's brother, Philip, danced for King Herod at his birthday party. He promised with an oath (horkos) to give her whatever she wanted as a gift in exchange for her performance. Little did he know that she had conspired with her mother to have John the Baptist beheaded! When he heard her request, he was sorry or very uneasy. Why was he uneasy? He was grieved because he made a promise with an oath or restricted himself to a certain punishment before the gods. The Bible says that he went ahead and commanded John to be beheaded. He did this for "the oath's sake" or because he declared the oath, especially in front of all his colleagues. In his heart, he wanted to take back his oath, but he couldn't. It wasn't culturally sound to do so, especially for a king. Like they say, "The king's word becomes law."

Now imagine God, our great king, being so angry at the Israelites that He bound Himself to a punishment if He allowed the Israelites to enter His rest. They definitely were not going to make it in! Fortunately for us, He was only angry with that generation. God remembered His oath-swearing covenant with Abraham and allowed the generation that was born in the wilderness to have an opportunity to make it in. God was bound by two oaths: The first to Abraham, that his seed would inherit the promised land, which they did; and the other, that this disobedient generation would not enter His rest, which they didn't. God was obligated to and yet fulfilled both promises.

THE FEAR OF GOD

In the book of Hebrews, we find that it is a dreadful thing to fall into the hands of the living God. (Hebrews 10:31) In fact, Jesus went so far as to say, "Do not be afraid of those who kill the body, and after that have no more that they can do. But I will show you whom you should fear: Fear Him who, after He has killed, has power to cast into hell; yes, I say to you, fear Him!" (Luke 12:5) Disobedience is dangerous, because it demonstrates a lack of the *fear of God.* I'm not talking the kind of fear of the Lord that only means to worship or reverence Him. It is the kind of fear that respects God, acknowledging not only His desperate love toward us, but also His ability to consume unbelievers with the fire of His wrath!

Unlike the popular side of Christianity that does not believe that God ever gets angry, I believe that He can get quite upset. Just ask Cain; or the Israelites; or Hopni and Phinehas; or King Saul. Do you need New Testament examples? How about Ananias and Sapphira? After lying about their promised giving to the church, they reneged on the full amount. They thought they were lying to Peter, but in actuality they lied to the Holy Ghost and died on the spot. Scripture goes on to say that "great fear" came upon all the church and upon all who heard about it. (Acts 5:11) Imagine in our opinionated, selfish, Americanized churches today how many people have reneged on their giving. Great fear would come upon us all if God was to commence the act toward us as He did with Ananias and Sapphira. There would be more dead carcasses than there were in the wilderness! It would be more catastrophic than Katrina, the Pacific Ocean tsunami and 9/11 combined! Should it take an enormous, nationwide church catastrophe in order for the fear of God to re-enter the church?

I also wonder if God is angry with those who teach a distorted concept of prosperity. It is the kind of prosperity teaching that manipulates, intimidates and abuses laity while the money-hungry preachers run rampant in material gluttony. Their teaching lacks balance. It defies true stewardship and economic empowerment. It always expresses the supernatural seed planting while never mentioning the practical applications of financial management. Trust me, I believe in both. I believe that God can place His "super" upon our "natural" and give us bountiful harvest from sincere seed planting. The Bible clearly states, "Give and it shall be given unto you: in good measure, pressed down, shaken together, and running over shall men give unto your bosom." (Luke 6:38) At the same time, I am confident that He likes for us to also apply meaningful, practical solutions to our everyday financial responsibilities.

Ironically, when we see people who promise great wealth without any Biblical soundness and swindle "seed" from the ignorant, who treat planting seed like scratching a daily lotto ticket (and are probably in desperate need of financial management classes), we tend to applaud and celebrate them instead of reproving and avoiding them. 1 Timothy 6:5 warns us concerning these "harvest hypnotizers," who suppose that godliness is a means of gain. Paul tells us to withdraw ourselves from them.

The fear of God is the recognition of the severity of the consequences of separation from God and living a life apart from Him, i.e., the second death, which is eternal torment in the lake of fire and brimstone. However, the fear of God is balanced with the recognition of His goodness toward us, especially the fact that He has given His only begotten Son, Jesus Christ, for us, to reconcile us back unto Himself and to put His life in us (regeneration) so that we can live a new, abundant life (flowing with milk and honey), a life that desires to draw near to God and to please Him.

> "Well said. Because of *unbelief* they were broken off, and you stand by faith. Do not be haughty but *fear*. For if God did not spare the natural branches, He may not spare you either. Therefore consider the goodness and severity of God: on those who fell, severity; but toward you, goodness, if you continue in His goodness. Otherwise you also will be cut off. And they also, if they do not continue in unbelief,

will be engrafted in, for God is able to graft them in again." (Romans 11:20-23 emphasis added)

INIQUITY WORKERS

When the fear of God is missing, the church casts off restraint. People begin to do things more wicked than the world does. Their concept of grace becomes distorted, holiness is a byword and spiritual power is manipulated for personal recognition. Jesus called this kind of unbelieving believers "Iniquity Workers." (Matthew 7:23) In fact, He tells them, "I don't even know you!" They may prophesy, do miracles and even win souls to Christ, but because they "work iniquity," Jesus will reject them. This is serious business here. The word used for iniquity is *anomia*, which means "the condition of being without law: lawlessness." It is a condition that demonstrates refusal to acknowledge God. It is a rebellious condition. Lawlessness is the condition characteristic of unbelief. It is the direct opposite of righteousness, which is the condition characteristic of genuine faith. Hebrews 1:9 demonstrates that there was a choice made to love righteousness and hate lawlessness. It is a decision of the heart to go in one direction of life or the other. You cannot enter God's rest nor have a life flowing with milk and honey while living in a condition of lawlessness.

Jesus punished these hypocrites with an everlasting banishment from His presence: "Depart from Me." The reason for their punishment is clear; they "worked" iniquity. The Greek verb used in this passage for work is *ergazomai*, meaning to labor, to do business, commit or perform. I'm starting to visualize that Jesus was specifically talking to people whose rebellion was an occupation. What do I mean by this? It was not necessarily the babe in Christ who kept slipping into fornication or using profanity or struggling with alcoholism that Jesus was referring to, but rather those who held a seat of influence in the Lord's kingdom business: the ones who prophesied, cast out demons and performed miracles. These were the ones whom the Lord called Iniquity Workers. They were doing the Lord's work deceitfully, preaching themselves and not Christ, and sought their own success and not His glory. They cashed in on the praises of men and exploited the innocent while seemingly doing the Lord's work. Sin was trivialized, disregarded and treated as harmless or neutral so that they could excuse themselves to indulge in it. However, Jesus likened them unto a foolish carpenter who built his house on sinking sand and not on a solid foundation. (Matthew 7:24-27)

There is little difference between the iniquity workers, harvest hypnotizers and the unbelieving Israelites of the wilderness. As a result of their condition and actions, they provoked the wrath of God and were restricted from entering God's rest. It is of great importance that the fear of God is instilled in us. The fear of God is the wisdom we need to endure our wilderness. Without it, we will wander for years and ultimately die in the desert and the stench of our dead carcasses will cause the fowls of the air to feast in victory over our unbelief. Let's be like the wise carpenter who built his house on a solid rock. When life's storms raging against us, we will not fall!

CHAPTER 6

Enter Into His Rest

SUPERNATURAL ENTRANCE

An entire generation failed to enter the land of promise. However, two men from the Exodus generation were privileged to enter the promised land. These men were persistent in their faith and believed what God had promised them. When spying out the land of Canaan, these two men brought back a faith report that was totally against the negative report of the majority. These men were committed to the revelation of God given to them by their prophet, Moses. They did not deter from the vision. These men, Joshua and Caleb, are examples of those who "caught" the vision. I believe that the way into God's rest is tied into your commitment to the revelation of God given to you through the man of God who covers you. Joshua and Caleb did not miss out on what God had in store because they defied the majority and obeyed the voice of him who spoke on behalf of God for their lives. Their obedience led them into the entrance of God's rest and they became the successors of Moses' vision, leading the next generation with them. Because of their obedience, the younger generation could trust the necessary instructions of Joshua and Caleb in guiding them into the promise that Moses so declared in their ears.

DON'T GET IT TWISTED!

Although their obedience was a key component in their approval from God to enter the land of promise, it still took the hand of God to get them beyond the Jordan River. Obedience always gets God's attention and approval. Obedience is the highest form of worship. Thus, it is the obedient worshiper whom God seeks or finds interest in. Oftentimes, it is this kind of worship that leads to the Jordan River of life. The Jordan River is the way out of wilderness living and the way into the promised life. However, the Jordan River was symbolic of that which impedes natural progress. At the brink of the Jordan, man finds his human strength and capabilities at a limit while realizing that there are certain things that only God is capable of doing. There isn't anything in man's power or nature that can cause him to penetrate the spiritual Jordan, not even his obedience. The word of God says, "Not by might, nor by power, but by My Spirit, says the Lord of hosts" (Zechariah 4:6). It will take something supernatural to help anyone progress past life's Jordan. It would take divine assistance to bring him into the realm of sustained blessings. Entrance into God's rest is based on God's approval and His divine ability to bring you into a realm that you have no right or permission in your humanity to access. Too often, Satan manipulates good-hearted people to begin to trust in their own obedience for their success. But instead, depend solely on His approval and love for you, rather than on your own obedience. Isaiah proclaims that "ALL our righteousness (obedience) is as filthy rags." (Isaiah 64:6) Sometimes we wonder why we do all the "right things" and still end up "messed up." Perhaps it is because we are lured into the same snare that many God-pursuers fall into, the snare of self-righteousness. Our doing the "right thing" begins to take the place of God. As the youth of our church may say, "Don't get it twisted!" Let His love and your love for Him always be your intent in obeying Him.

God instructed the people to sanctify or prepare themselves because on the following day they were going to cross over their Jordan into the land flowing with milk and honey. As with Moses and the departure out of Egypt, it took the hand of God to part the Red Sea. It was God who saved them from Egypt with a great deliverance as they made preparation by following the instructions of sprinkling the blood of an unblemished lamb upon the door of every Hebrew home so that the death angel would pass by. Their preparation led to the outcome of God's supernatural intervention. And now with Joshua, for departure out of the wilderness, it takes the hand of God to surpass the Jordan. Again, they had to prepare themselves according to the word that proceeded out of the mouth of God. All exits and entries into spiritual dimensions require divine assistance, especially that of entering the overflow. Abundant living takes the human participation of spiritual preparation and obedience but not without the hand of God giving His divine support. "The eyes of the Lord move to and fro throughout the earth *that He may strongly support* those whose heart is completely his" (2 Chronicles 16:9 NASB). The Father is seeking a dedicated person who He can strongly support or support with His mighty hand.

SPIRITUAL DIARY

A well-overlooked divine instruction and principle is mentioned here in Joshua 4. God instructed Joshua to select a man from each tribe who would lay stones in the Jordan River as a memorial for future generations to see. There have been countless men of faith who stepped into the realm of God's rest, yet leaving no memorial stones, no chronicle or diary of what it took for God to move on their behalf. It is sad to see spiritual achievers with no successors. Some have died hiding their heritage with themselves in their grave. Mantles are in the graveyard, riches have returned to worldly hands, while many children of faith are left spending a lifetime trying to find out how to live more productive Christian lives, both spiritually and financially.

It reminds me of the question Gideon posed to the angel of the Lord, "Where be all his (the Lord's) miracles which our fathers told us of?" (Judges 6:13)

Little did Gideon know that sin and disobedience are what often hide the evidence of God's hand (Judges 6:10). Memoirs of faith have been destroyed by ungodly men intercepting and disrupting the lineage of spiritual achievers. For instance, after Joshua, Israel went on a rollercoaster ride of obeying and disobeying God. By the time Gideon came on the scene, God's people were in blatant disobedience again. So great was their disobedience that God allowed them to suffer torment by the Midianites. For seven years, the Midianites swept across Israel, destroying their crops and their livestock. They were literally and strategically destroying Israel's source of wealth. This is why the angel found Gideon threshing wheat in a winepress. He was trying to hide it (his source of wealth) from the Midianites. Maybe God chose to anoint Gideon to deliver His people because at least he was trying to salvage an inheritance for the next generation.

Paul instructs Timothy to commit the Gospel, which he heard of him, to faithful men who would be able to teach others also. (2 Timothy 2:2, italics added.) It is very important that we become faithful and develop sincere, faithful people in the faith. We need successors who can carry the Word of God forth when we are long gone. As God moves you into a life flowing with milk and honey, you have to make sure you find believer(s) to whom you can pass the baton of spiritual and material resources so they can continue the legacy of Jesus Christ.

EVIDENCE OF GOD'S POWER

God desires for us to leave evidence of His life. Scripture says, "That ye may *prove* what is that good, and acceptable, and perfect, will of God." (Romans 12:2) The evidence of God's power at work is key to people fearing God (Joshua 4:24), not only His people but also those of the world. When Joshua sent spies into the promised land, he sent them to Jericho, where they met a woman by the name of Rahab. She said to the spies, "I know the Lord hath given you the land, and that *your terror* is fallen upon us, and that all the inhabitants of the land *faint because of you.* For we have heard how the Lord dried up the water of the Red Sea for you, when ye came out of Egypt; and what ye did unto the two kings of the Amorites...and as soon as we had heard these things, *our hearts did melt.*" (Joshua 2:9-11, emphasis added)

The people had "mad respect" for Joshua and the boys. Why? It is because of the evidence of the power of God. When people see and hear about the power of God, it commands respect. A good indication that you have stepped into God's rest is the respect that you command, not demand, from others because of the power and favor of God on your life. Have others heard of what God has done for you? As a matter of fact, what has he done for you lately? What is your latest testimony? Paul said, "Knowing therefore the terror of the Lord, we persuade men." (2 Corinthians 5:11) Rahab said that the people were so terrified because of what God had done for Israel and of the possibility of what He could do to them if they stood in His way. Are there any demons afraid of what God would do on your behalf? When you're living a life flowing with milk and honey, it will command the respect of demons. Just ask Jesus!

When the Amorite and Canaanite kings heard that the Lord had dried up the Jordan for the Israelites to pass over, "their heart melted, neither was there spirit in them any more, because of the children of Israel." (Joshua 5:1) The more God does for you, especially supernaturally, and people hear about it, the more you will command respect. What God does for you should be the talk of the town, not for your ego but for His glory. The children of Israel were tallying up success stories and their enemies were breathless! This is how you want the demons of hell to respect you. You want them to be so frightened at your manifested relationship with God that they will fear and tremble at your presence. It's time to start counting up and journaling our success stories in God. It's better than collecting stamps for the rest of your life!

GILGAL- The Place of Trust

After the commemorative stones were set at Jordan's brinks, more divine instructions were given at a place called *Gilgal*. Two instructions were of major importance to God before He allowed them to possess the land. Entering and possessing the land are two different things. They were in the land, but not possessors of the land. God's objective at Gilgal was to give them a conquering spirit. In order to do so, He had to "roll away the *reproach* of Egypt." (Joshua 5:9) This is where Gilgal receives its name, which means "rolling away."

The Hebrew word for *reproach* is *cherpah*, meaning "a disgrace, or a condition of shame." In Chapter 4, I briefly shared that the reproach of Egypt was the fact that Israel suffered 400 years of slavery only to find themselves wandering 40 more years in the wilderness as though their God was nowhere to be found. First, they were the laughingstock of nations because of their shameful slavery in Egypt. Then their merry-go-round wilderness fiasco added to their disgrace.

Here in Gilgal, unbeknown to Israel, the sound of their successes was heard abroad, whereas the same people that scorned them for their previous debacles now were intimidated by their ability to come out of their failures with transformed resilience. God was rolling away their reproach the moment He miraculously brought them into another realm of life. Gilgal is a variation of the Hebrew verb *galal*, which means "to roll away or to roll upon." I find it very interesting that this word also carries the meanings "to commit" and "to trust." Psalms 37:5 says, "*Commit* (galal) thy way unto the Lord; trust also in him; and he shall bring it to pass." Psalms 22:8 says, "He *trusted* (galal) on the Lord that He would deliver him." Gilgal is a place of trust and commitment. Not only was God rolling away the reproach of Egypt, but the people were to roll themselves upon God. They were to commit themselves to and trust God. To *commit* means *to wholly dedicate or devote oneself to another.* To *trust* means *to place total confidence and dependence in someone.* Commitment and trust in God is needed to possess a life flowing with milk and honey. It is the kind of commitment and trust needed for instructions given by God which may seem at times illogical to human reasoning. In gaining a conqueror's spirit, you will have to submit to commands that may often defy your intellect and logic. Possessing a life flowing with milk and honey is contingent upon our ability to accept and follow the "illogical" commands of the Most High. In the military, it is not up to us to understand the strategies of the general, but simply for us to carry them out. So it is with God. We don't have to always understand His instructions. We just have to fulfill them. That's our responsibility as good soldiers, not only to endure hard trials but even hard instructions.

CIRCUMCISION OF THE HEART

In rolling away the reproach of Egypt, God commanded the acts of circumcision and Passover to be performed. Circumcision and Passover were promises of devotion and dependence. They were rituals performed in response to the promises of God of His providential care that He would keep eternally for them. This new generation of believers had never experienced either ordinance, which now had to be put into practice once again.

The ceremony of circumcision is the removal or cutting away of the foreskin of the male reproductive organ. This act of devotion was originally instructed by God to Abraham in Genesis 17 as a sign of the covenant in which He declared that He would "give unto thee...the land of Canaan, for an everlasting possession." (Genesis 17:8) It was a covenant of possession. It was Israel's reminder of their right to possess. The circumcision gave them confidence in God to pursue His promise without fear. This is the spirit of the conqueror.

Circumcision was to serve as an outward sign of inward dedication to God. In the New Testament, Paul sheds greater light on the subject of circumcision, for things of the Old Testament were types pointing to the reality of life in Christ. Paul writes, "For he is not a Jew, which is one outwardly; neither is that circumcision, which is outward in the flesh: but he is a Jew, which is one inwardly; and circumcision is that of the heart, in the spirit, and not in the letter; whose praise is not of men, but of God." (Romans 2:28-29)

Circumcision is a matter of the heart, "in the spirit." The cutting away of the flesh of the male foreskin was only a type of the cutting away of the flesh in the heart, that is, carnality. We call this "sanctification." Today, if you mention sanctification in the church, you are almost looked upon as though you used profanity. In some church circles, if you talk about sanctification, you are held in suspicion of being legalistic. It's quite the opposite. *Sanctification* is a setting apart of one's life to be wholly dedicated to divine use. "If a man therefore purge himself from these, he shall be a vessel unto honor, *sanctified*, and meet for the master's use, and prepared unto every good work." (2 Timothy 2:21) Circumcision of the heart, or sanctification, is an indication that you are ready to conquer the enemy and possess a life flowing with milk and honey. Circumcision of the foreskin of the reproductive organ carries the spiritual implication that the promises of God will never come about through flesh (carnality). The promises of God will always come about through the Holy Spirit.

KEEP THE FEAST – THE PASSOVER

Another interesting instruction given in Gilgal was the reinforcing of Passover. The Passover ceremony was to commemorate the deliverance of Israel from Egyptian bondage. In Exodus 12, the Lord instructed Moses and the Israelites to slay an unblemished lamb and apply the lamb's blood upon the doorpost of every home so that the angel of death would pass over them when he saw the blood. Again, this ceremony was a foreshadowing of Christ being the perfect Lamb of God that was slain for the sin of the world. (John 1:29, 36) Not only do we acknowledge this truth, but we "keep the feast" by living lives of sincerity and truth. (1 Corinthians 5:8) This is another expression of sanctification. We ought to purify our hearts and live honestly and genuinely before God and man. This is a sign of someone living a life flowing with milk and honey. Both the Passover and circumcision were signs of commitment and trust in the Lord and His continual care for His people. *Sincerity and integrity are marks of a life of someone ready to conquer and possess all that God has promised them.* A conquering spirit requires us to "keep the feast." To possess the promises of God, we must "keep the Passover." The Passover helps us to have a heart that will reflect on God's deliverance of us out of the bondage of sin and shame. The Passover implies that we can look forward to God delivering us into a life flowing with milk and honey, i.e., God's rest. It's time to conquer and possess!

CHAPTER 7

He Will Exalt You

"Go; view the land, especially Jericho." (Joshua 2:1)

There is much significance in why Jericho was chosen to be the first
stronghold conquered by Israel. Not taking away from the fact that
it was the closest large city to their point of entry into Canaan,
known as the city of palm trees (Deuteronomy 34:3), which provided an oasis for those coming out of the wilderness, but its name
provides a clue as to its priority. Jericho is known as one of the
oldest inhabited cities on Earth[14] and could have been the source of
much of Canaan's sinful activity. This compels me to believe that it
was first on God's hit list to punish the Canaanite (Amorite) sins
that were now "full." (Genesis 15:16) From the Lord's perspective,
the hourglass of Canaanite sins had expired and it was time to fulfill
the prophecy, which he promised to Abraham and his seed; first up
– Jericho. It was due time. It was a divinely strategic time. It was an
epoch, history-making and eventful time. It was an accurate, precise
moment when the prescribed prophecy was to be fulfilled. As
planned, it was the fourth generation. (Genesis 15:16) Time and
prophecy collided into fulfillment.

The name Jericho, Hebrew *yarichow*, taken from *yareach*, means
"its moon or moon city." Named after the Canaanite god *Yarih*
(possibly the same as the Mesopotamian god *Sin* and the Babylonian
god *Chemosh*), the moon god to whom they worshiped, the people
of Jericho erected what would be known as the strongest city in
Canaan. It covered about eight acres, with walls 30 feet high and 20
feet thick and was considered to be invincible. The inhabitants of
Canaan attributed this invincibility to the power of Yarih. Out of all

the gods of the pagan Arab world, the moon god was exalted as the "highest" of all, i.e., the *Most High*.

MOST HIGH GOD

Jericho appears to be the battle over who the real Most High God is. Battling over whose God is greater or who has the right to claim certain names and status was not uncommon. For instance, in Elijah's day, the battle was over whose God was the God of prosperity and rain. The confrontation was between Yahweh and Baal. Jezebel and her false prophets had convinced the majority of Israel that Baal was why they were so prosperous. When their hearts and minds were turned toward Baal, God sent his prophet Elijah (whose name consequently means "God IS the Lord"). Sending a man whose name means "God is the Lord" is a good indication that He was ready to pick a fight and put an end to all the Baal nonsense. Of course, you know the outcome – victory for Yahweh. Maybe this is why Scripture declares that the battle is not ours, but the Lord's.

Now, in Jericho, God was ready to battle over who was Most High. He was only 40 years removed from defeating the gods of Egypt when He demonstrated His power against them with the 10 plagues. I call the battle of Jericho "the second battle of exaltation." The first battle of exaltation was in heaven against Lucifer.

> "How you are fallen from heaven, O Lucifer, son of the morning! How you are cut down to the ground, you who weakened the nations! For you have said in your heart: I will ascend into heaven, I will exalt my throne above the stars of God; I will also sit on the mount of the congregation on the farthest sides of the north; I will ascend above the heights of the clouds, I will be like the Most High." (Isaiah 14:12-14)

Lucifer said in his heart:

- I will ascend into heaven
- I will exalt my throne above
- I will also sit on the mount
- I will ascend above the heights
- I will be like the Most High

Lucifer cunningly persuaded one-third of the stars (angels) to follow him in his insurrection. And there they went: one-third of heaven's angelic population along with the prime minister of pride, Lucifer, now called Satan, falling like lightning from heaven. When anyone tries to exalt themselves, it is called pride, and wherever pride is, there will always be something ready to fall. Satan wanted to ascend above, exalt himself and be like the Most High!

Throughout Scripture and history, the name "Most High" or "(El) *Elyon*" was often attributed to Yahweh. Here are a few instances from Scripture:

> "Then Melchizedek king of Salem brought out bread and wine; he was the priest of *God Most High*. And he blessed him and said: 'Blessed be Abram of *God Most High*, Possessor of heaven and earth; and blessed be *God Most High*, who has delivered your enemies into your hand.' And he gave him a tithe of all." (Genesis 14:18-20) This was when Abraham was blessed by Melchizedek after he rescued Lot in the battle of the kings.

> "The Lord thundered from heaven, and *the Most High* uttered His voice." (2 Samuel 22:14) This was part of a song of David after the Lord had delivered him out of the hands of all his enemies and from the hand of Saul (v. 1).

"That they may know that You, whose name alone is the Lord, are *the Most High* over all the earth." (Psalms 83:14) This was part of a prayer to frustrate a conspiracy against Israel.

"It is good to give thanks to the Lord, and to sing praises to Your name, O *Most High*; to declare Your lovingkindness in the morning, and Your faithfulness every night." (Psalms 92:1-2)

"For You, Lord, are *most high* above all the earth; You are exalted far above all gods." (Psalms 97:9)

"I said, 'You are gods, and all of you are children of *the Most High.*'" (Psalms 82:6)

In Daniel 3:26, King Nebuchadnezzar calls Meshach, Shadrach and Abednego out of the fiery furnace, proclaiming them to be "servants of the Most High."

In Daniel 4:32-34 and 5:21, Daniel receives the interpretation of King Nebuchadnezzar's dream in which he was going to wander from among man and be with the beasts of the field until he knew that *the Most High God* rules in the kingdom of men and gives it to whomever He chooses. After Nebuchadnezzar's depraved vagabond experience, he finds himself giving praise to Jehovah as the Most High.

In Daniel 7:18, 22, 25, 27, we are called "saints of the Most High." And would you believe it, Satan is trying to "wear us out"?

Perhaps the most familiar passage of Scripture is found in Psalms 91:1: "He that dwelleth in the secret place of *the Most High* shall abide in the shadow of the Almighty." This psalm is attributed to Moses, who wrote it while in the wilderness. This is an indication that during their wilderness saga, the Israelites were already acknowledging YHWH (Yahweh or Jehovah) as Most High. Thus, at the battle of Jericho, the name El Elyon was a household name to

Joshua and the Israelites. And how dare someone else lay claim of this name to their god!

SUPER-LOGICAL INSTRUCTIONS

For the destruction of Jericho and their moon god, God gives Joshua an unusual instruction to march around the city once for six days without making any noise, no shouting nor blowing the ram's horn. But on the seventh day, they were to march around the city seven times and the seven priests bearing the ram's horn shall blow the horn. And when the priests shall make a long blast with the ram's horn, the people were to shout a great shout.

Would it not have been easier for them to just speak and command the walls to tumble down? What about, "Let's just pray and watch God move"? Why did they have to march around the city a total of thirteen times? This appeared to be illogical. What I admire about Joshua is that he didn't complain; he simply obeyed.

What we call illogical is logical with God. I believe there to be a reason behind everything God says or does. Instead of looking at the hard-to-fathom instructions as illogical, we should look at them as "super-logical." When Jesus turned water into wine or fed 5,000 people with two fish and five loaves of bread, we didn't call it unnatural, but supernatural. If miracles are supernatural, then His instructions are super-logical.

It's easier to obey an instruction that is super-logical than to think of it as illogical. What we have to keep in mind is that God knows things that we don't know. This being the case, He may instruct us beyond our knowledge. This is where faith, trust and humility have to kick in. This is where the preparation in the wilderness and the consecration at Gilgal meet God's timing for accomplishment. Joshua's trust, humility and obedience was matched up with an epochal moment that all rested upon a super-logical instruction. This is the equation for exaltation. It is when all of your preparation meets a significant event that requires your obedience to a super-logical instruction. It's all arranged and staged by a divine purpose.

The ill-mannered envy of brothers, sudden slavery and unjust imprisonment by foreigners was Joseph's preparation to be exalted. His epochal moment was when Pharaoh had a disturbing dream. His super-logical instruction was to walk right into Pharaoh's chamber and not only tell him what he dreamed the night before, but also what it meant. "Why not just show mercy and put it on the heart of the king to let me out of prison?" Joseph could have questioned. "After all, the hearts of kings are in Your hand." No, God knew something Joseph didn't know. He knew that He was going to bless him to become the second-in-charge of all Egypt. He knew that the famine would force his jealous brothers to come to Egypt for food and to repent before him. He knew that this was what God had established to fulfill the dream that He gave Joseph when he was a little lad. He knew it had to take Joseph meeting the king face-to-face and speaking words to him that only the king and God Himself knew in order to exalt Joseph and move him from that horrible dungeon and into the palace to redeem his brothers and to advance God's name on Earth.

The everyday stench of sheep dung, warding off wolves, fighting and killing lions to protect his father's flock was the grooming ground of exaltation for the unnoticed, harp-playing shepherd boy David. His epochal moment was when he found himself one-on-one with a more-than-9-foot-tall giant (the Bible gives his height as six cubits and a span, about 9½ feet), Goliath, who was mouthing off in deplorable defiance against the entire military of Israel and their God. God's super-logical instruction was for David, a young teenager, to take an *ephah* (22 to 23 quarts) of dried grain, 10 loaves and 10 cheeses to his brothers and their captain to a battleground and see how they were faring and to bring back news. David could have questioned God, "Why not send someone from the battlefield to give my daddy a report, like Job had servants that were bearers of bad news?" Or better yet, why not ask God to give Goliath a heart attack or plague him with emrods (boils) like He had done to the Philistines on one other occasion? Why make David carry food to his brothers and see Israel's well-respected army cowering at the voice of one man? Or since David was going to the battlefield to fight, at least inform him and give him some armor or at least a military uniform to make him look like someone who's ready to fight. God knew something David didn't know. He knew that this was the battle that would bring David high respect with the people. He knew that He led David there to eventually become Saul's musician and chief adjutant, befriending Jonathan, Saul's son, who would teach him the ways of the palace, not knowing that David was the next king of Israel. What he sent the prophet Samuel out to Bethlehem to anoint David for was the anticipation of David's obedience at the dangerous valley of an intense battlefront with only a slingshot and a family picnic basket with wheat bread and high-cholesterol cheese.

HE WILL EXALT YOU

Joshua's wilderness experience and Gilgal consecration prepared him for this epochal event at Jericho. He placed unwavering trust in God, followed his super-logical instruction thoroughly and the walls of the greatest stronghold in history were crushed into powder by a march and a shout!

God is preparing you for an epochal moment in your life in which He is so willing to exalt you. You now have the kingdom equation in mind. Start focusing on your wilderness training and see it as a period of great preparation to be a possessor of a life flowing with milk and honey. Let it develop your humility, trust and obedience. Your Jericho, your Goliath or your moment in the Pharaoh's chamber is bound to come. Will you be ready to follow God's super-logical instruction thoroughly? The Exalted One desires to exalt you.

> "Today the Lord has proclaimed you to be His special people, just as He promised you, that you should keep all his commandments, and that *He will*

set you high above all nations which He has made, in praise, in name, and in honor, and that you may be a holy people to the Lord your God, just as He has spoken." (Deuteronomy 26:19, italics added)

Unlike Satan, who tried to exalt himself above, we read here where Moses shares with the people that God Himself desires to set them "high above all" kinds of people (nations).

I find it interesting here in Deuteronomy 26:19 that Moses uses the adjective *elyon* for "high above." So the Most High, Elyon, exalts us by placing part of who He is in us. For instance, when God wanted to anoint us, He put His anointing in us – "Christ (the name that expresses anointing) in us, the hope of glory." So when He wants to exalt us, He places Elyon in us. And when Elyon gets on the inside of us, there is nothing that can stop our lives from being significant. Moses made a great discovery that helped him in his wilderness experience: the secret place of the Most High. People who find that secret place eventually get Elyon all over them and their lives become significant on Earth for the kingdom of God.

"Humble yourselves (feel very insignificant) in the presence of the Lord, and *He WILL exalt you* (He will lift you up and make your lives *significant*)." (James 4:10, Amplified Bible) The New Century Version translates this verse, "Don't be too proud in the Lord's presence, and *He WILL make you great.*"

"Therefore humble yourselves under the mighty hand of God, *that He may exalt you in due time.*" (1 Peter 5:6) The Message Bible translates this verse, "So be content with who you are, and don't put on airs. God's strong hand is on you; *He'll promote you at the right time.*" The right time is that epochal moment.

From these various translations, we discover God's desire to exalt you, promote you, give you honor and make you great. That was the promise that He gave Abraham. A life flowing with milk and honey is a life that is honored and exalted by God Himself.

OVERTAKEN BY BLESSINGS

"Now it shall come to pass, if you diligently obey the voice of the Lord your God, to observe carefully all His commandments which I command you today, that the Lord your God will set you high above all nations of the earth. *And all these blessings shall come upon you and overtake you,* because you obey the voice of the Lord your God." (Deuteronomy 28:1, italics added)

When God "elyons" us, or sets us high above, He does it by pouring out great measures of blessings. What is a blessing? A blessing (Hebrew *barakah*/Greek *eulogia*) is a bountiful gift or present, prosperity, praise or treaty (agreement) of peace (shalom). When God blesses you, He endows you with praise (a high level of recognition/honor), prosperity (wealth) and makes an *agreement of shalom* (agrees to make you well or whole in every area of your life)! Many have simply defined "blessing" as the empowerment to succeed. Since God is the one who is distributing the blessing, it is He from whom our success comes and not of our own ability. The barakah (blessing) is supernatural. It is a God-doing. This is why Paul declared, "We have this *treasure* in earthen vessels, that the excellence of the power may be of God and not of us." (2 Corinthians 4:7) That treasure or bountiful gift in you is of God and not of yourself.

The blessings shall "come upon" us. The Hebrew word for "come upon" is *bow'*, which means "to light upon, be brought to, be introduced to, or to go towards." With these definitions in mind, I am convinced that when God gives a blessing, it is deliberate and with direction. There are places in the Word of God where God commands a blessing. The blessings have no choice but to obey God in His deliberate instruction for it to introduce itself to a particular person. The Septuagint (the oldest Greek translation of Hebrew Scripture) parallels the Hebrew *bow'* with the Greek *heko*, which means "to seek intimacy with one, become his follower, or to come upon one unexpectedly." I like to say that the blessing is love struck and seeks its lover out in order to be intimate with them. It begins to follow and stalk its lover with infatuation and unexpectedly shows up like a man surprising his lover with flowers and a variety of gifts. When God exalts you, He is going to cause blessings to fall in love with you. This is the *rest* from and of God.

God's blessings will not only come upon us, but they also will "overtake" us. The Hebrew word for "overtake" is *nasag*, which means "to reach, to be able to secure, to become sufficient or to have enough." Its Greek Septuagint parallel is *heurisko*, which means "to recognize, detect, or find a thing sought for." Thus, the kind of blessings which God releases will not only fall in love with us and give us bountiful gifts, but they will also be like a responsible husband and secure us, make us feel safe and at peace, and confident that we will have a sufficient supply of anything we will ever be in need of. The blessings will not only be in love with us but they will walk down the aisle with us in holy matrimony and promise to be with us all the days of our lives. This is why David could declare, "SURELY, goodness and mercy shall follow me all the days of my life…" (Psalms 23:6) *God's rest, a life flowing with milk and honey is a life living in the realm of sustained blessings.* When God commands the barakah to come our way, it will come with lasting commitment to see us succeed in life. Barakah always recognizes and detects people who are obedient to God, those who observe to do ALL that God instructs, whether the command is simple or super-logical. Have you made yourself attractive to blessings? Are you ready for blessings to marry you?

JESUS WAS HIGHLY EXALTED

"Have this attitude in yourselves which was also in Christ Jesus, who, although He existed in the form of God, did not regard equality with God a thing to be grasped, but emptied Himself, taking the form of a bond-servant, and being made in the likeness of

men. Being found in appearance as a man, He
humbled Himself by becoming obedient to the
point of death, even death on a cross. For this reason also, *God highly exalted Him,* and bestowed on
Him the name which is above every name, so that
at the name of Jesus EVERY KNEE WILL BOW,
of those who are in heaven and on earth and under
the earth, and that every tongue will confess that Jesus Christ is Lord, to the glory of God the Father."
(Philippians 2:5-11)

This passage of Scripture shows us how Jesus humbled Himself
and was eventually highly exalted by the Father. In humbling
Himself, Jesus first "emptied" Himself. This means that He stripped
Himself of His heavenly position and authority, while remaining
God; but He became a Man through the virgin birth and grew up
having to rely on the assistance of heaven. He had to become fully
man in order for redemption to be legal. The apostle John records
that Jesus was given the Holy Spirit without measure. Finally, He
humbled Himself by becoming obedient to the point of death, even
death on a cross. He knew the divine purpose for leaving heaven
was to be a perfect (without blemish/sin) living sacrifice and die on
behalf of mankind for our redemption. He knew that death was the
price of redemption, and He obeyed the super-logical instruction of
the Father until His final breath had expired on the old rugged cross
on Golgotha's hill.

Through Jesus' obedience, sacrifice and humility, God "highly
exalted" Him. The Greek word used here for "highly exalted" is
huperupsoo, which means "to exalt to the highest rank and power; to
raise to supreme majesty." Huperupsoo was used only one time in
Scripture and it was only used of God highly exalting Christ. God
raised Jesus to the highest seat of authority ever. Ephesians 1:20
says "He (God) sat him (Jesus) at His own right hand in the heavenly places." When Jesus was raised from the dead, He proclaimed,
"ALL power (Greek *exousia* – authority) is given unto me in heaven
and in earth." After His ascension, Jesus was given the honor of

being seated with the Father. This highly exalted position empowered Christ to have authority "far above principalities, powers, might and dominion." (Ephesians 1:21) This refers to Jesus having authority over all classes and ranks of angelic beings, i.e., spiritual creatures. His name is above (more excellent than) every name, in this world and in the world to come (Ephesians 1:21), and at the name of Jesus EVERY knee shall bow, of things in heaven, of those things on earth, and things under the earth; and EVERY tongue shall confess that Jesus Christ is Lord. (Philippians 2:10-11) God has put ALL things under Jesus' feet and gave Him to be the head over ALL things to the church.

The most interesting part about the exaltation of Christ is that it was "to the glory of God the Father." It honored God to have exalted Christ. Isaiah said "it pleased the Lord to bruise (Hebrew *daka'*, "to crush") Him." (Isaiah 53:10) He suffered disdain and scorn and was rejected and abandoned. He was a man of severe pains and became acquainted with injuries (grief). His agony in the garden, His being betrayed, His battered face, severe scourging and torture at the cross pleased the Father because this was the only price for redemption. Jesus was willing to pay the price of His own life in order to reconcile us back into a right relationship with the Father. For this reason and because He fully obeyed, Jesus was highly exalted. And when the Father highly exalted Jesus, it brought glory and honor to the Father. Though it pleased the Father to bruise Jesus, the Father counts it a great honor to have highly exalted Jesus as well. Jesus' death, burial, resurrection and atonement glorified the Father to the fullest extent, because it openly illustrated, with honor, the ultimate attributes of the Divine nature and His immeasurable love.

SEATED WITH HIM

"And hath raised us up together, and made us sit together in heavenly places in Christ Jesus." (Ephesians 2:6)

Through the full obedience of Christ in reconciling us to the Father, He gave us access and a right to the kingdom of God, for we "sit together in heavenly places." This signifies a seat of authority. Believers have a seat of authority that is quite often unoccupied and vacant. This vacancy of our spiritual authority is because of our ignorance of how we are raised up. We realize that He has forgiven us of our sin but fail to see that He raised us up to a powerful, abundant life like unto His own. We are blindsided by the misinterpretation of the Gospel. The attitude of some toward grace is as sin-filled as some without it. Some people take out of context the freedom of grace to excuse their unchanged, unregenerate lifestyle while claiming a right to eternal life. Whether they are truly saved is not my argument, but rather that if they continue in this attitude and belief, they will never discover the real joy and life that grace has to offer.

A life of sitting together in heavenly places in Christ Jesus is preceded by our being raised up together with Him. You cannot be raised up until you have died. I'm not talking about being raised from being "dead in sin" but being raised after you are "dead to sin." Romans 6:1-2 says, "What shall we say then? Shall we continue in sin that grace may abound? Certainly not! How shall we who *died to sin* live any longer in it?" (italics added) We have to die to sin, which means our old nature has to be subjected and crucified (daily). Jesus says, "Whosoever desires to come after Me, let him deny himself, and take up his cross *daily*, and follow Me." (Luke 9:23, italics added) Where are we following Him to? Answer: heavenly places. We should have an attitude of hatred toward sin like God does and a heart after right living and purity of heart and desiring to do those things which please the Father. For if it pleased the Father to bruise the Son, we should be thinking that with our suffering, through trials as well as daily crucifying of self, the Father would also receive pleasure through our trials like He did with Christ. Thus, this is the indicator that you are raised up together with Christ and are ready to sit together in heavenly places. In other words, you are ready to be exalted by God. "This is a faithful saying:

for if we died with Him, we shall also live with Him. If we endure, we shall also reign with Him." (2 Timothy 2:11-12a)

When He raised us up, He also made us to sit together in heavenly places, places of rule and dominion. Believers need not live beneath their authority but should walk in it. We have privileged power and the right to exercise it on the earth and in the spirit realm against everything that opposes God. We realize now that worldly, carnal "old man" living restricts us from living in the authority that we have in Christ Jesus. Life in God's rest is a life that is no longer restricted by the unsuppressed, uncrucified old man. Rather, it is a life that presents itself daily as a living sacrifice, holy and acceptable to God for divine service. (Romans 12:1) Only the new man who is created in Christ Jesus is able to access the realities of kingdom authority. *Living in God's rest is living in heavenly places in Christ Jesus.*

When you live in this God-exalted position, which every Christian can obtain, you don't need earthly titles and positions to validate and esteem you. Earthly affirmation and confirmation from peers and affiliates has its place but it is meaningless without true spiritual authority. I am appalled to say that we have too many people with earthly titles but empty spiritual seats. Too often our altar calls are powerless and plastic with too many people falling backwards (or pushed down) and not falling forward on their faces before a holy God. Thank God for the ones who have filled their spiritual position first and was confirmed on earth afterward. There is a seat in heavenly places in Christ Jesus waiting to be filled by you. Remember, *it gives God glory when He can exalt any of His children.*

CHAPTER 8

Shalom - Living In God's Rest

LIVING IN HIS REST

"Mark the *blameless* man, and observe the *upright*; for the future of that man is *peace (shalom)*." (Psalms 37:37 emphasis mine)

As we enter into the realm of God's rest, conquering and possessing our Jericho (and other places of spiritual symbolism in the promised land), we must also learn to *live* in God's rest. I have coined the phrase "a *life* flowing with milk and honey" from the very thought of *living* in God's rest. *Living in God's rest expresses a life that has continuity in the presence of God.* It is a person who has learned to utilize the priceless resource of God's authority. As I mentioned in Chapter 1, God's rest (katapausis) is authority over life's storms. In addition to giving you His authority over life's storms, He also gives you His authority to *rule* your heart. We call this authority, this ruling power, "Shalom."

> "Let the *peace (shalom)* of God RULE in your hearts…let the word of Christ (the rain of heaven) dwell in you richly." (Colossians 3:15-16 emphasis mine)

The purpose of Shalom is to bring you into wholeness. That's exactly what Shalom means. It is God's wholeness manifest.[15] While the New Testament Greek word *eirene* is influenced by the Hebrew word *shalom*, our English word "peace" gives an inadequate definition for both eirene and shalom. I mentioned in the Introduction of this book that *shalom* means *"completeness (wholeness), soundness, health, safety, wellness, prosperity, and peace."* Thus, *it carries the idea of being well in every area of your life.* This is *God's wholeness manifested in the life of the believer.* Their hearts have a deep and rich indwelling of the word of Christ which influences who they are. They have *soaked in the rain of heaven* allowing it to rule their very being. Now they can carefully deliberate their thoughts to make precise kingdom decisions, implementing His plan in their daily lives.

Shalom is God's wholeness visible in the life of the believer with the blessings and promises of God materialized (or being materialized) from consistent obedience to God's instructions in every dimension of their lives.

Shalom is soundness. Soundness is a word that ideally pertains to inward stability that comes from a correct belief (acceptance and conviction of truth, which is Christ and His Holy Word). It is the inward life of a man that is "spiritual." As a result, he lives out what he believes. The Bible uses words like *godly, righteous, holy, perfect, just, upright, and blameless* to describe the man who is sound. A common word that we often use to explain King James' usage of the word "perfect" is "mature." Keep your eyes on the *mature* man and thoroughly observe him. David guarantees that this blameless (mature) man has a promising future of shalom. He has a guaranteed future of being well in every area of his life. The prophet Jeremiah reveals this promise of shalom, "I know the thoughts (plans) that I think towards you, plans of peace (shalom) and not of evil, to give you an expected end (promising future)." (Jeremiah 29:11 emphasis mine) The upright, blameless man "minds the things of the Spirit" and is considered to be "spiritually minded."

> "For to be carnally minded is death, but *to be spiritually minded is life and peace (shalom)*." (Romans 8:6,

emphasis mine) I personally interpret this Scripture verse to imply that *being spiritually minded (minding the things of the Spirit) leads to a Shalom-life or a life of wholeness.*

"You will keep him in *perfect peace* (absolute shalom), whose *mind* (inward life) is stayed on You, because he trusts in You." (Isaiah 26:3 emphasis mine)

Shalom is *health*. It is being influenced and constantly abiding by God's dietary plan and other health instructions that leave your body in good physical shape and restricts the possibility of diseases.

Shalom is *prosperity*. It is applying the principles of the kingdom to your finances as good stewards over what God allows you to manage. He progressively rewards you with more (abundance). The Bible informs us that if we are faithful over a few things God will make us ruler over many." (Matthews 25:21)

"Let the Lord be magnified, who has pleasure in the *prosperity* (shalom) of His servant." (Psalms 35:27)

Shalom is *safety and peace*. As we live continually in God's presence and under the influence of His Spirit, He protects us and causes our enemies to retreat and dare to attack us without suffering great ruin.

"Do not touch My anointed ones, and do My prophets no harm." (1 Chronicles 16:22)

"And the peace (shalom) of God, which surpasses all understanding, will *guard* (protect) your hearts and minds through Christ Jesus." (Philippians 4:7, emphasis mine)

"When a man's ways please the Lord, He makes even his enemies to be *at peace* with him." (Proverbs 16:7 italics added)

"I will both lie down in *peace* (shalom) and sleep; for
you alone, O Lord, make me dwell in *safety*."
(Psalms 4:8 italics added)

Shalom rules the heart making a person complete in character,
sound in spirituality and doctrine, physically healthy, financially
advancing as a good steward, and socially at peace with your fellow
man. Shalom means that kind of peace that results from being a
whole person in right relationship to God and to one's fellow man.[16]

THE GOD of SHALOM

Several passages of Scripture reveal God as being "the God of
peace (shalom)." Gideon built an altar and named it Yahweh
Shalom (The Lord is our peace) (Judges 6:24). Below are more
Scripture passages that declare God as the God of peace:

> "Now may *the God of peace* Himself sanctify you
> completely; and may your whole spirit, soul, and
> body be preserved blameless at the coming of our
> Lord Jesus Christ." (1 Thessalonians 5:23 emphasis
> mine)

> "Now may *the Lord of peace* Himself give you peace
> always in every way (in every dimension of your
> life). The Lord be with you all." (2 Thessalonians
> 3:16 emphasis mine)

> "Now may *the God of peace* who brought up our Lord
> Jesus from the dead, that great Shepherd of the
> sheep, through the blood of the everlasting cove-
> nant, make you complete (whole) in every good
> work to do His will, working in you what is well
> pleasing in His sight, through Jesus Christ, to whom

be glory forever and ever. Amen." (Hebrews 13:20-21 emphasis mine)

"The things which you learned and received and heard and saw in me, these do, and *the God of peace* will be with you." (Philippians 4:9)

"Finally, brethren, farewell. *Become complete.* Be of good comfort, be of one mind, *live in peace* (shalom/wholeness); and *the God of love and peace* will be with you." (2 Corinthians 13:11 emphasis mine)

"Now *the God of peace* be with you all. Amen." (Romans 15:33)

"And *the God of peace* will crush Satan under your feet shortly. The grace of our Lord Jesus Christ be with you. Amen." (Romans 16:20)

In fact, the Bible says that God Himself is our peace (shalom) (Ephesians 2:14.). There is no true peace without Him. Jesus is called the Prince of shalom (Isaiah 9:6) who came to bring this shalom on Earth (Luke 2:14) and to guide our feet into the way of this shalom (Luke 1:79). He did this by presenting His kingdom (which is a kingdom of peace (Romans 14:17)), and preaching a gospel of shalom (Romans 10:15, Ephesians 2:17). In John 14:27, Jesus says, "Peace (shalom) I leave with you, My peace (shalom) I give to you; not as the world gives do I give to you." It is His peace, His shalom. Christ gives us Shalom, which to me, is a part of Himself. "These things have I spoken unto you, that *in Me* you might have peace." (John 16:33) It is "in Him" that we may experience shalom. Shalom is the presence of the Holy One. This Shalom is literally His "wholeness" manifest.[15]

SEEK SHALOM

> "Depart from evil and do good; *Seek peace* (shalom)
> and pursue it." (Psalms 34:14 italics added)

God told the high priest that when he declares the blessing over the lives of the children of Israel he must declare, "God will give you shalom." (Numbers 6:16) I am solely convinced that this is why the apostle Paul saluted the church with "grace and peace (shalom)" in all of his epistles. Perhaps, as Biblically scholastic as Paul was he was mindful of the instructions given to the Old Testament high priest to declare it over the lives of God's people.

We are told by King David to "seek shalom and pursue it." In this passage of Scripture, to "seek" is the Hebrew *"baqash"* which means "to seek to find; to seek to secure; to desire, ask, or request." David is writing this in light of all the afflictions and troubles of life (life's storms).

From the Hebrew definition we find that asking and desiring are two essential aspects of seeking. First, there is *"desire."* It is unlikely that you would pursue anything without a desire (craving/passion) for it. Your desire gives you the drive you need to chase after something; in this case, it is shalom. Many Christians do not have continuity in God's presence that will allow them the grace of obtaining His shalom because they have no desire for it. David is challenging us to desire shalom, crave for to have it and live in it.

Asking for shalom is another part of our pursuit of it. The Israelites were commanded to pray for the peace (shalom) of Jerusalem. Asking is an essential part of seeking. Imagine travelling to a country that you have never been to before. As you arrive at the airport terminal, I would think that the most logical thing to do is "ask" someone for directions to your hotel or place of stay. Perhaps there would be plenty of questions that you would have to ask during the entire travel arrangement until you secure your destination. "We have not, because we *ask* not." (James 4:1)

Shalom is to be sought after until it is found and secured. I like that the Message Bible translates this verse, "Embrace peace -- don't let it get away!" We should continue in our desire for and asking for shalom until it becomes visible evidence that we have embraced it, secured it, and are living in it daily. This is God's rest revealed, embracing shalom, God's wholeness and living in it everyday. Like Joshua and Caleb, it is going after the promise of a life flowing with milk and honey. It is enduring your wilderness and letting your disobedience die, while developing a lasting obedience and love for God, crossing over life's Jordan and entering into that realm of rest. It is not only entering into His rest but living in continuity of His presence conquering your giants, subduing your Jericho, and possessing your inheritance.

CHAPTER 9

If You Come, You Can Rest

COMMANDED TO COME

> "*Come* unto Me all ye that labour, and are heavy laden and I will give you *rest*. Take My yoke upon you, and learn of Me; for I am meek and lowly in heart: and ye shall find *rest* unto your souls. For My yoke is easy and My burden is light." (Matthew 11:28-30, italics added)

In this passage of Scripture, Jesus unlocks the secret of how to obtain His rest. The compassion of Jesus was elevated to a point of fiery demand as He looked at the weary, burdened people who had been depleted of strength to live and survive. He looked out amongst the crowd of hearers and onlookers and saw insomnia and fatigue. Satan had gotten the best of humankind, which made Jesus all the more determined to release the greatness of His ability to resurrect life in them. He proclaims to all present a solid promise of rest. Let's probe deeper into this Scripture for insight on how to receive God's rest.

First, we have the word "come." Dictionary.com defines the verb "come" as "*to approach* or move toward a particular person or place; *to draw near*." The Greek word for "come" is *deute*, which means "come hither; come here; interjection, come! Or come now!" The imperative mood of this word corresponds to the English imperative and expresses *a command* to the hearer to perform a certain action by the order and authority of the one commanding. Thus, "Come unto Me…" is not at all an invitation, but an absolute command requiring full obedience on the part of all who hear. We are commanded to come to Him to receive His rest.

Secondly, the types of people that He was commanding to come were the ones that labored and were heavy laden.

First, we have those who "labour(ed)." The Greek word used here for labor is *Kopiao*, which is a derivative of *kopos*, which means "a beating; a beating of the breast with grief or sorrow." Thus kopiao insinuates a person grown weary, tired, depleted and exhausted with grief and the pressures of life.

In addition to the laborers, we have those who were "heavy laden" (which is actually one Greek word, *Phortizo*). Phortizo carries the idea of someone loading your back with burdens as a farmer would do to his beasts of work. It means to weigh down. Metaphorically, it means to load one with a burden of rites and unwarranted precepts. Thus, Jesus was implying possibly two things here: (1) Sometimes we let people wear us down with their opinions of us or the feeling of pressure as a result of trying to live up to the expectations of others (especially religious expectations) and what others feel we ought to be accomplishing or how we should be living; and (2) we sometimes weigh down our own hearts and minds with trying to fulfill laws rather than simply walking intimately with our God. This leads to being burdened and weighed down because we often forget that no one can live up to the Law without breaking it and that our righteousness is not of ourselves but is by the blood of Jesus Christ and His redemptive work on the cross and an intimate, growing relationship with our God. As a result of trying to live up to the Law, when we fall short of it, the weight of guilt, shame and condemnation becomes unbearable. Thus, we are laden with heaviness and the mask that we wear becomes heavier than Goliath's armor.

If we neglect to hear and obey His command (not merely an invitation) to *come*, we would continue to live in taxing tiredness, exhausted over life and struggling to make God and ourselves satisfied by living according to rules and not a relationship, trying to fulfill precepts rather than pleasing a Person (the Father). We will always be pressured by the expectations and opinions of others rather than experiencing the clemency and compassion of a loving God. Until we obey His command to come to Him, we will continue to hide behind the heavy mask that conceals the things that weaken our ailing hearts. To neglect His command is disobedience and a denial of His passionate concern for our crippled condition.

If we hear His command to come unto Him and absolutely obey it, we will experience the fresh, rejuvenating power of His Rest, "...and I will give you rest." (v. 28) The word that Jesus uses for "rest" in this passage of Scripture is the Greek word *Anapauo*. Anapauo (from *Anapausis*) is taken from two Greek words, *Ana*, meaning "into the midst," and *Pauo*, meaning "a pause or stoppage; a ceasing from." Thus, Anapauo means "into the midst of a pause." It means to *refresh* or to cause or permit one to cease from any movement or labor in order *to recover and collect his strength*.

An Old Testament parallel of this Scripture is Isaiah 40:29-31:

> "He gives power to the weak, and to those who have no might He increases strength. Even the youths shall faint and be weary, and the young men shall utterly fall, but those who wait on the Lord shall renew their strength; they shall mount up with wings like eagles, they shall run and not be weary, they shall walk and not faint." God's rest is a renewal of strength and only the everlasting Giver of life, who neither faints nor gets weary, can replenish strength. (Isaiah 40:28)

HOW TO "COME TO HIM"

Here are several ways that we can demonstrate our obedient response in coming to Him:

•

(1) REPENTANCE

In Acts 17:30, we are told that God has "commanded men every-where to repent." The Greek word for repent is *Metanoeo* – "to change one's mind for the better, heartily to amend with abhorrence of one's past sins."

In his book Intercessory Prayer (pp.162-163), Pastor Dutch Sheets, when explaining "letting in the Light" (which is true revelation of Jesus), defines Biblical repentance, Metanoia (a derivative of Metanoeo), as having "a new knowledge or understanding" – a change of mind. He uses the analogy of a camera to illustrate true repentance.

> The word "light" in 2 Corinthians 4:4 is *photismos*, which means "illumination." It is similar to another word in Ephesians 1:18, "enlightened," which is the word *photizo* – "to let in light." We can almost see the English words "photo" or "photograph" in these Greek words; they are, indeed, derived from them. What happens when one takes a photo? The shutter on the camera opens, letting in light, which brings an image. If the shutter on the camera does not open, there will be no image or picture, regardless of how beautiful the scenery or how elaborate the setting.
>
> The same is true of the souls of humans. And this is exactly what is being said in these two verses in 2 Corinthians 4. It sounds like photography language. It makes no difference how glorious our Jesus or wonderful our message, if the veil (shutter) is not removed, there will be no true image (picture) of Christ. Oh, sometimes we talk people into a salvation prayer without a true revelation (unveiling), but there is usually no real change. That is why fewer than 10 percent – I've heard figures as low as 3 percent – of people who "get saved" in America

become true followers of Christ. The reason is that there is no true Biblical repentance, which only comes by Biblical revelation.

Repentance does not mean to "turn and go another way" – a change of direction. That's the Greek word *epistrepho*, often translated "converted" or "turn" and is the result of repentance. Repentance (metanoia) means to have "a new knowledge or understanding" – a change of mind.

In Biblical contexts, repentance is a new understanding that comes from God through an unveiling (revelation). It is the reversing of the effects of the Fall through Adam. Humanity chose their own wisdom, their own knowledge of good and evil, right and wrong. Humanity now needs a new knowledge – from God. Paul said in Acts 26:18 that he was called "to open their eyes" – enlightenment, unveiling, revelation, repentance – "so that they may turn (epistrepho) from darkness to light."[17]

Open up the shutters of your heart so that the glorious light of the Gospel of Jesus can shine in! Then you can truly repent (have a metanoia experience) from the unveiling of His glory and receive a new knowledge and understanding that will cause you to change. Your entire being and life will turn from that old, dark image of self and evil, toward the glorious Light of Jesus Christ. That is repentance! That is a "coming unto Me (Him)!"

Jesus and John the Baptist both preached repentance for the purpose of receiving the kingdom of heaven that has now come to everyone. (Matthew 3:2, 4:17; Mark 1:15, 6:12; Luke 13:3, 5) The kingdom of heaven here references the power of God and salvation. The result of repentance led to salvation, faith, healing, casting out devils, miracles and the like. People were receiving rest from their weariness!

"The Lord is not slack concerning His promise…but is longsuf-fering toward us, not willing that any should perish, but that all should come to *repentance*." (2 Peter 3:9)

"The goodness of God leads thee to *repentance*." (Romans 2:4)

Repentance helps you find rest because it initiates your relation-ship with God and dissolves the guilt and shame of sin as you find forgiveness and healing through the grace and love of Jesus Christ.

(2) "DRAWING NIGH" THROUGH CLEANSING AND PURIFYING

"Draw nigh to God, and He will draw nigh to you. Cleanse your hands, ye sinners; and purify your hearts, ye double minded." (James 4:8)

From the viewpoint of wanting Christians to recognize their friendship with the world (James 4:4), the apostle James identifies two types of "worldly" Christians and what they must do to dissolve their friendship with the world that ultimately opposes God. Friendship with the world must be eradicated as we are drawing near to the Father. James classifies these world-friends as (1) sinners and (2) double-minded.

First, the sinners (Greek *hamartolos*) are those who are *devoted to sin*. They are heinous or habitual sinners, morally wicked. They simply enjoy the pleasures of living carnally, not really desiring true fellowship with God. James commands a cleansing of the hands. The hands are expressive of works, deeds, conduct, lifestyle, etc. James commands the habitual "Christian" sinner to clean up his life! James uses the Greek verb *katharizo* (from *katharos*) for cleanse, which means to free yourself from every corruption and falsehood; to be sincere and genuine; innocent, blameless; to be free from corrupt desires, sin and guilt. Descriptively, it is like a vine cleansed by pruning and thus made fit to bear fruit. As long as we are heinous, habitual sinners, we cannot bear much fruit in Christ.

The apostle John, when speaking of the True Vine (Jesus) and its branches (believers) says that if the branches do not bear fruit, they are cut off, but for the ones that are bearing fruit, the Vinedresser (the Father) prunes them in order for them to bear more fruit. (John 15:1-2) Ideally, the spiritual pruning process is the cutting away of sinful practices. We are promised that as we are being pruned or cleaning up our lifestyle, we will be drawing near to God. God's rest is revealed in the pruning process and becomes evident through fruit in the believer's lifestyle as he is drawn closer to the Father.

Next, we have the double-minded man. The Greek word used to define double-mindedness is *dipsuchos*, which translates as "having two souls." The soul is often depicted as that part of man that is the seat of the mind, will and emotions. Thus, dipsuchos carries the idea of being divided in what you think is best for yourself, having a divided interest, and wavering between two opinions or ideas. It is not so much having an intellectual doubt as it is doubt about commitment. The double-minded man cannot commit his way to the Lord. Basically, the heart of the double-minded is torn in two. The double-minded man is unstable in all his ways. (James 1:8) In other words, he lacks integrity, steadfastness, stability or consistency. He is too fickle, unpredictable and indecisive. I like how John Bunyan, in his book Pilgrims Progress (the 7th Stage), gave character to the double-minded man by naming him "Mr. Facing-both-ways, a kinsman to Mr. By-End from the town of Fair Speech."

Jesus taught on the impossibility of serving two masters (Matthew 6:24; Luke 16:13), hating the one while loving the other. You cannot serve God and Mammon. The Lord wants us to make a defining decision whether to serve Him or the other gods (idols). Jesus also taught that we have to be single-hearted toward God (Matthew 6:22; Luke 11:34). David and Paul expressed their single-heartedness toward God in announcing their "one thing" attitude. (Psalms 27:4; Philippians 3:13)

James instructs the double-minded man to purify his heart from having a divided interest that results in a lack of commitment, if he desires to draw near to God. I find it interesting that James uses the Greek word *hagnizo* for "purify." It is a word originally used when a person is making something pure for ceremonial purpose or even purifying himself through ceremonial rituals like in Old Testament times. Thus, it signifies consecrating something to God as sacred or holy through devotion. Hagnizo is a derivative of the word *hagos*, which means "a thing full of awe (dread and wonder) or something to be cherished with tender love." This is what happens when someone devotes a person or thing to God as holy; they view it and cherish it as precious and valuable to God, and to desecrate it would be awful (full of awe). The heart that is devoted to God has been given to Him as a treasure, belonging solely to Him. The Apostle James is implying that the double-minded person, when approaching God, should consecrate and devote (purify) his heart to God as a treasured, sacred thing so valuable that to renege or tamper with it would bring about a terrible consequence. "He that hath this hope in Him will *purify himself* even as He is pure." (1 John 3:3)

An indicator that a person has purified their heart may be found in 1 Peter 1:22, when Peter commends the saints for "*purifying your souls in obeying the truth* through the Spirit unto unfeigned love of the brethren." The believers demonstrated a sincere, heartfelt, authentic love toward one another as a result of devoting their hearts to God as a sacred treasure solely for Him.

We approach God by being cleansed, pruned and purified from a sinful lifestyle and from a divided heart. The promise is that if we draw nigh to Him, He WILL draw nigh to us! At the same time, we find an antidote for the spiritual malady of worldliness. We will find God's rest as we cleanse and purify ourselves through the Word of God and communion with the Father through the Holy Spirit.

(3) CRYING UNTO THE LORD

> "Now it happened in the process of time that the king of Egypt died. Then the children of Israel groaned because of the bondage, and they *cried out*; and *their cry came up to God* because of the bondage." (Exodus 2:23)

As they sense a window of opportunity opening, a glimpse of hope following Pharaoh's death, the Israelites approached God by means of "crying out." Pharaoh was the personification of their bondage, limitation and hindrance. It was under his rule and decree that taskmasters were assigned to make their bondage more rigid and burdensome. When he died, it was as though for a moment the Israelites had a chance at freedom. And what better way to get God's attention than to cry out for His assistance? The Bible says that their cry "came up to God." They approached God with a cry.

Their cry was so strong that God *remembered* His covenant *and acknowledged (favored, paid close attention to) them*. (Exodus 2:24, 25). In fact, the Greek Septuagint parallels the Hebrew word for "cry," *tsa'aqah* with the Greek *krazo*, which literally means "to croak like a raven." Smith's Bible Dictionary says that the smell of death is so gratifying to the raven that when passing over sheep and a tainted smell is detected, the raven begins to cry very loudly.[18] In other words, when the raven senses its prey, the nearer it gets, it cries all the more with passionate fervor until its hunger is satisfied. This is how God looked at His people. He found a body of burdened believers crying out in passionate hunger for Him because they sensed that their season of progressing toward His rest had now come!

As a result of their cry, God released Moses from His kingdom conversation at the burning bush, commissioning Moses to free His people as a response to hearing their cry. (Exodus 3:8)

The same is true with us if we cry out to the Father. He will intervene on our behalf and help us.

> "For you did not receive the spirit of bondage again to fear, but you received the Spirit of adoption by whom we *cry out*, Abba, Father." (Romans 8:15, italics added)

> "Likewise the Spirit also helps in our weaknesses. For we do not know what we should pray for as we ought, but the Spirit Himself makes intercession for us with *groanings* which cannot be uttered." (Romans 8:26, italics added)

We will run into God's rest through our crying out and "groaning" approach toward Him and He will deliver us from the evils inside and outside.

> "The righteous *cry out*, and the Lord hears, and delivers them out of all their troubles." (Psalms 34:17)

(4) WAITING UPON THE LORD

In Isaiah 40:31, we have another secret on how to respond to Jesus' command "come to Me" in order to receive His rest. Isaiah says that our "strength" can be renewed, which is just like the rest that Jesus promised when we obey the command to come to Him, i.e., a recovery of our strength.

Isaiah says, "They that *wait* on the Lord." How can I wait and come at the same time? This isn't your normal sit-around-and-not-do-anything kind of wait. Instead, it is an action word. The Hebrew word used here for wait is *Qavah*, which means "to look eagerly for, to hope, to expect, to linger for." It also means "to collect or to be collected; to gather." The Greek Septuagint translates qavah by using the Greek *hupomeno*, which means "to tarry, to remain, to abide; to not recede or flee; to endure, to bear bravely and calmly." Hupomeno is derived from the root verb *meno*, which not only means "to remain and abide" but also (when speaking of persons) "to remain as one; not to become another or different; to survive or live."

This implies surviving through every obstacle and hardship by doing whatever it takes to get into and remain in the presence of God. It speaks of doing every activity that is necessary to maintain the presence of God in your life until He shows up with His strength and infuses it into your heart. This renewing of strength is a supernatural impartation and can only be received by looking for and expecting God to move. It takes unwavering faith to endure distractions without flinching. You refuse to recede or relent until your strength has been recovered by God Himself. It may take extra worship time, additional praise or extending yourself over and beyond the normal routine of prayer. It may take giving up your "me-time" for "more-of-Him-time." It may take fasting, turning down "special" events and turning off favorite television shows, and even giving up spending time with familiar friends. When your back is against the wall and your strength has been depleted, it is not the time to collapse and have a pity party; rather, it is the right time to bravely put off everything else in order to command heaven to rush to your rescue with overflowing strength.

> "And let us not grow weary while doing well, for in due season we shall reap if we do not lose heart." (Galatians 6:9)

(5) PRAISE

Another way of approaching God is through praise. *Praise* is the multifaceted act of expressive celebration of the Lord Jesus Christ. Praise is essential to approaching the Lord. In fact, He promised to inhabit the praises of His people. (Psalms 22:3) The intent of praise is to lift up (honor) the person esteemed worthy of it in the hope that someone else would recognize the value of the one being celebrated. This is why some Hebrew words for praise signify a "boasting." God is to be bragged about. We should brag about His goodness, mercy, salvation, lovingkindness, favor, power, character and name. Several passages of Scripture charge us to "make your boast in the Lord" or "magnify Him." He is just that good!

Psalms 100 reveals the relationship between praise and approaching God:

> "Make a *joyful noise* unto the LORD, all ye lands. *Serve* the LORD with gladness: *come* before his presence with *singing*. Know ye that the LORD he is God: it is he that hath made us, and not we ourselves; we are his people, and the sheep of his pasture. *Enter* into his gates with *thanksgiving*, and into

his courts with *praise*: *be thankful* unto him, and *bless* his name. For the LORD is good; his mercy is everlasting; and his truth endureth to all generations." (Psalms 100:1-5, italics added)

The Psalmist (David) challenges us to "come" before the presence of the Lord and to "enter" His gates. Simply put: approach God. Even more so, the actual word for presence is "face." So David inspires us to get in God's face, figuratively, of course! Approaching God is getting face-to-face with Him. David cites ways to get into the presence of the Almighty King. He uses words like *singing, thanksgiving, being thankful, praise and blessing Him*. Each of these is a form of praise, but there are slight differences in their meanings. Let's examine more closely the different Hebrew words used for praise in Psalms 100 so that we can get a better understanding of how to approach God:

- **A joyful noise.** This is actually one word in Hebrew, which is *ruwa`*. It means "to shout, to raise a sound, to shout a war cry." It is also used in Joshua 6:5 when God told Joshua to instruct the people, while marching around the city of Jericho, to "shout with a great shout; then the wall of the city will fall down flat." I am convinced that supernatural activities can happen when we "raise a sound" before God. There is a sound, a shout from the depths of our hearts that God looks for. I'd like to say that a "joyful noise" is a sound that pleases God. I call it a "faith shout," because Joshua and the Israelites had to ruwa` before one brick ever moved from Jericho's massive wall. They had to believe the superlogical instruction that somehow, when they let out a great shout, that Jericho's walls would tumble down. It's a sound that says, "I believe it is done before it happens."
- **Singing.** This Hebrew word, *rananah*, means "a ringing, joyful cry." In today's terms, it may translate to "repeated, cheerful outbursts," like when a favorite sports team wins a game and the fans begin to cheer because of the victory.

Rananah is derived from *rannan*, which literally means "to overcome." I'd like to say that rananah is a distinctive praise of one who just fought through a hard struggle and overcame. It's not just any old song you're singing, but it's *the spontaneous, cheerful outburst of an overcomer!* We must come before His presence with cheerful outbursts more convincingly than cheering for our favorite football team.

- **Thanksgiving.** We must enter His gates with "thanksgiving." It is the Hebrew *towdah*, which means "*confession*." Towdah means "to agree with God," to say what He says about Himself, about you and about your situation, no matter how it looks. We enter His gates by confessing what He says.
- **Praise.** This particular Hebrew word for "praise" is *tehillah*, which is derived from the root *halal*, meaning "to be boastful, to celebrate, and to flash forth light." We must come into His courts boasting and celebrating His character, attributes, power and name. When we praise God this way, we send forth flashes of light into the atmosphere and possibly to those whose minds have been overwhelmed by the darkness of sin and evil, convicting them (and ourselves) of the awesomeness of God.
- **Thanks.** This is the Hebrew word *Yadah*, which means to shoot arrows, to cast out or extend (the hands). It is associated with towdah. Thus, as we extend our hands, we confess who God is to us and loudly announce our appreciation of Him and what He has done (and is doing) for us.
- **Bless.** The Hebrew *Barak* means "to kneel as an act of adoration." Kneeling signifies yielding. When I kneel before Him, I am yielding my mind, emotions, conscience and heart to Him so that He may do as He pleases.

When we praise God, we approach Him and enter His presence and are we are made secure with His rest. In His presence, there is fullness of joy. (Psalms 16:11) Joy is the result of entering His presence.

(6) DILIGENTLY SEEKING (FAITH/BELIEVING)

Hebrews 11:6 says,

> "Without faith it is impossible to please God. He that cometh unto God must believe that He is and that He is a rewarder of them that *diligently seek* Him." (KJV, italics added)

The author of the book of Hebrews also gives us a revelation on how to come to God. He says that we "must believe that He is." At first glance, this seems to be an understatement. It may appear that the author of Hebrews is merely implying that we should accept the fact that there is a God who exists. But this is far from the meaning of this statement and it would contradict the meaning of true faith in God. However, when the author continued with "and that He is a rewarder of them that diligently seek Him," he brought light to the statement "must believe that He is" and the kind of faith necessary in coming unto God. It is the "diligently seeking" faith. When we approach God, it must be a genuine, devoted effort to find Him.

The Greek word *ekzeteo* is used here in Hebrews 11:6 to describe the kind of person that God will reward for approaching Him. Ekzeteo means "to seek out, search for, seek carefully, investigate, scrutinize, to beg, crave, to demand back, to require, demanding something from someone." So much can be interpreted from this definition. If I can just consolidate it to a working definition, I would say that an ekzeteo believer is "one who is conscientiously investigating God, tracking His moves, hunting Him down, pursuing Him, soliciting and desperately demanding and asking anyone and everyone he possibly can for clues (revelations) about Him, carefully scrutinizing, studying and dissecting every word and fact in hopes of fulfilling the craving, hunger and yearning that he has of apprehending the very person who has captured his entire life's attention." This is how God wants us to approach Him, and according to the author of Hebrews, it is a "must." The apostle Paul puts it this way: "I keep *pursuing* it in the hope of taking hold of that for which the Messiah Yeshua took hold of me." (Philippians 3:12, the Complete Jewish Bible)

Isaiah says, "*Seek the Lord* while He may be found, call upon Him while He is near." (Isaiah 55:6, italics added)

God rewards the *ekzeteo* (diligently seeking, must-find-God) believer. The reward: His rest, an abundant life, a life flowing with milk and honey - shalom.

(7) WORSHIP

It is not unusual to find worship used almost synonymously with praise, especially in our Western way of thinking. We have somewhat dumbed down worship to a Sunday morning praise service when, in essence, it is much more than that. Our culture has lost the meaning of true worship and that meaning must be recaptured if we are to live in God's rest.

Harold Best, in his book Music Through the Eyes of Faith, defines worship in the broadest sense as "acknowledging that someone or something else is greater – worth more – and by consequence, to be obeyed, feared, and adored...Worship is the sign that in giving myself completely to someone or something, I want to be mastered by it." (p. 143)[19]

Another clear definition of worship is by Warren Wiersbe, who writes, "Worship is the believer's response of all that they are – mind, emotions, will, body – to what God is and says and does." (Warren Wiersbe, Real Worship, p. 26).[20]

My working definition of *worship* is that "worship is a posture of the heart that settles on what is exclusively worthy of its greatest devotion and which causes the devotee to act out in expressions of loving obedience and service to reveal its stand."

In 2 Chronicles 16:9, Hanani the seer (prophet) reveals to King Asa that the Lord scans the entire earth in hopes of having the opportunity of finding someone He can strongly support. But He looks for a certain type of person – those who have a heart "perfect towards Him." (KJV) The NKJV uses "loyal to Him." NASB says "completely His." The NIV & NLT say "fully committed to Him."

This is worship. From this insight, I can see why the Lord says, "You shall have no other gods before Me" (Exodus 20:3) and "For thou shalt worship no other god: for the Lord, whose name is Jealous, is a jealous God." (Exodus 34:14) He wants your whole heart and nothing less.

Satan tried to tempt Jesus by saying, "All these things (kingdoms) will I give You if You will fall down and worship me." (Matthew 4:9) Satan was saying to Jesus, "Give me your greatest devotion and undivided service, the total commitment of your heart, and I will give you all the kingdoms of this world and their glory."

I like Jesus' response: "Away with you, Satan! For it is written, 'You shall worship the Lord your God, and HIM ONLY you shall serve.'" Jesus' total commitment and loyalty of heart was reserved exclusively for the Father, and He expressed His stand by sharply rebuking Satan after Satan's attempt to take it away.

Obedience is one way of acting out the posture of a committed heart. Obedience is worship. Bowing down and becoming prostrate was another way of expressing the complete loyalty of your heart to God. We sing the songs of falling down on our knees and bowing before His presence, but let's be real, how many Christians do you see at your Sunday morning "worship" service worshipping in this manner? After all, this is the most accurate physical posture before God that describes real worship. Everything else may be categorized as praise. Bowing the knee or lying prostrate (falling on one's face) was a physical demonstration of a totally yielded heart. If you went into the presence of a superior, such as a king, you could not just lift up your hands or merely shout "Thank you, King" and expect him to think that you were ready to obey him or were totally devoted or loyal to him. In fact, you may get killed or dragged out with many stripes. You must bow before the king!

The most common word used for "worship" in the New Testament is the Greek word *proskuneo*. It literally means "to kiss, like a dog licking his master's hand." What a way to define worship! If you ever had a dog as a pet, you know very well that the dog is fully aware of whom his master is and loves being in the presence of his master and expresses this love with hysterical leaps upon the master's lap followed by tons of licks on the master's hand. Worship of our Master, the One who has rightful ownership over us and whom we have yielded complete control to, is expressive, lively, high-spirited and passionate. It is never lethargic and dull. Have you ever seen a dog just look at his master as to say, "Yeah, I know you're just getting home from work, but I'll holla at ya later?" Not hardly. The dog knows the presence of his master. My dog, Favor, knows the sound of my car's engine distinctly from any other car in the neighborhood and is ready to sprint outside the house even if he is in the room farthest from the driveway and eager to show his affection and submission to me the moment he senses me pulling into the neighborhood. A dog knows his master, subjects himself to his master and shows him reverence by licking his master's hand – proskuneo.

We should approach or come to the Lord like a dog does his master. In this, He will give us rest. Genuine worship of the Father is rewarded with rest. The rest that we will receive is His presence, where there is fullness of joy. (Psalms 16:11) The Father seeks genuine worshipers, those who will worship Him in spirit and in truth. (John 4:23-24) He is looking for proskuneo*ers* whom He can strongly support.

8) COME BOLDLY

Hebrews 4:16 says,

> "Let us therefore *come boldly* to the throne of grace,
> that we may obtain mercy and find grace to help in
> time of need." (italics mine)

If there is ever a Scripture verse that has been misinterpreted, it is this one. So often have I heard people citing this Scripture while justifying their religious arrogance in "going to God," as though He will accept their selfish desires in spite of their skewed attitude and lackadaisical living. Can we put a demand on God? Does God owe us anything? Rather, I beg to say we owe Him everything.

This statement of "coming boldly" to the throne of grace was preceded by "therefore," which lets me know that it was because of a particular reason mentioned beforehand that we can come to God in this way. First, the author of Hebrews reminds us that the Word of God is living, powerful and sharp, piercing through the soul and spirit, and discerns our thoughts and intentions (v. 12). Secondly, he tells us that there is no creature hidden from God's sight, but all things are naked and open in the eyes of Him to whom we must give account (v. 13). And lastly, we have a High Priest (Jesus) who can relate to and sympathize with our weaknesses because He was in all points tempted as we are, yet without sin (v. 14).

According to these three things preceding it, "coming boldly" to the throne of grace obviously does not mean to "come arrogantly" to the throne of grace, as though God has to do something for us because we're Christians. Rather, it still gives us an overwhelming sense of gratitude for His ability to sympathize and identify with us and a sense of humility from knowing that God knows everything about us, inside and out, even the finest of details such as the number of hairs upon our head or the sinful thoughts which we don't want anyone else to know that we thought about. Catch my drift?

When the King James Version of the Bible translated the Greek *parrhesia* as "boldly," it became somewhat of a stumbling-block for misinterpreting how to approach God respectfully. *Parrhesia* means "unreservedness in speech; openness, frankness; without conceal-ment; confidence, assurance." The confidence is based upon relationship and knowing our place in the relationship. It is coming to God transparently. When you are transparent, you can be up-front, honest and frank, not hiding anything. This is how we can come to His throne of grace. When we come to God transparently, not trying to hide anything (as though we could), we receive mercy and grace to help us at the right moment in every situation. God gives His rest to transparent believers who come to Him.

Conclusion - Make Every Effort

"*Let us therefore be diligent* to enter that rest, lest anyone fall according to the same example of disobedience." (Hebrews 4:11)

REST RECAPPED

The Biblical meaning of "rest" is far more than getting a good night sleep every day. Throughout this book, I revealed the true meaning of God's rest for us, primarily by defining the three Greek words *katapausis, sabbatismos* and *anapauo.* Let me share these words and their definitions with you again:

- **Katapausis** means "a calming of the winds." The winds can represent any situation that may appear tumultuous and that causes great turmoil. When a person has entered God's rest, these winds are calmed. They can be tempered by the authority of Christ within the believer.
- **Sabbatismos** means "a keeping of the Shabbat (Sabbath)." The Sabbath was the most important day for the Hebrew. Shabbat means "to cease and desist from labor, and rest." The Shabbat was commanded by God and held in light of God's resting from creation on the seventh day. To the Hebrew, it means to stop creating and to enjoy the Creator and what has already been created for you. Sabbatismos was considered holy unto the Lord, and when it is not observed,

it is considered unholy and disobedience to the command-ment of the Lord.

- **Anapauo** (from Anapausis) is taken from two Greek words, Ana meaning "into the midst" and Pauo meaning "a pause or stoppage, a ceasing from." Thus, Anapauo means "into the midst of a pause." It means to refresh or to cause or permit one to cease from any movement or labor in order to recover and collect his strength.

It would be hard to have insomnia of any sort when living in God's rest. When we live in Christ, the heavens open up over us and we experience the abundant life He has planned for us, not the "good life" we attempt to make for ourselves. When we enter into His rest, we cease from our own works. (Hebrews 4:10) We lose great strength when toiling day-to-day trying to secure a good life for ourselves. Enact the power of God to calm life's storms, cease from your stressed-out working and recover your strength by coming to God. He has an abundant life for you, flowing with milk and honey, a realm of sustained blessings and a cessation of lack. He is anxious to bless you, exalt you, seat you in heavenly places, bring you to a life of wholeness, make you well in every area, and strongly support you when you surrender your total heart to Him.

MAKE EVERY EFFORT

Now that God's rest has been revealed, it is time for you to make a conscious decision to walk in that revelation. God's rest is available for you.

I mentioned in the previous chapter how to receive God's rest and that is, of course, by "coming" to Him through repentance, cleansing and purifying ourselves, crying out to Him, waiting upon Him, praising and worshiping Him, diligently seeking Him, and coming open and transparent before Him.

God promised us rest. He sent His Son not only to make a pub-lic announcement about it, but also to give us access to it, which He did when He died on the cross for our sins, reconciling us to the Father.

It is left up to us. The writer of Hebrews admonishes, "Let us therefore *be diligent to enter that rest*, lest anyone fall according to the same example of disobedience." (Hebrews 4:11, italics added)

The author of Hebrews tells us to "be diligent" to enter God's rest. He uses the word *spoudazo*, which means "to exert oneself, endeavor, labor, study, or *to make every effort*."

I like the Complete Jewish Bible version, which says, "Therefore, *let us do our best* to enter that rest, so that no one will fall short because of the same kind of disobedience." (italics added)

If we are going to work, let it be the work of "entering in." I call spoudazo "entering-in work." We should study, labor and exert all of our time and energy in our endeavor of entering in. Whether it's spending quality time in meaningful communication with God, aggressively seeking after Him through Scripture or in worship, meditating on a living word from God, exerting ourselves in sharing the good news of Jesus (and His rest), or thoroughly carrying out a God-given, super-logical instruction, let us exhaust all our energy, efforts, time and resources to enter into that REST that has been promised us. Let us do our best; let us spoudazo; let us do "entering-in work."

According to the author of Hebrews, if we do not spoudazo, we can fall into the same example of disobedience. Spoudazo is obedience. Making every effort and doing our best to enter into His rest is obedience. Joshua made every effort. Caleb made every effort. Others throughout history have made every effort to enter into God's rest. Now it's your turn. It is your turn to cease from creating and to enjoy the Creator and what He has created for you and what He is going to do for you. It is your turn to utilize the greatest resource given to mankind, which is the authority of Christ to calm life's storms. It is your turn to be refreshed and recover your strength so that you can do "entering-in work" and exert your energy toward living an abundant life flowing with milk and honey, living in sustained blessings.

Endnotes

Introduction

1.   www.wordnet.princeton.edu/per1/webwn
2.   www.en.wikipedia.org/wiki/insomnia
3.   www.lunesta.com/understandingInsomnia/understanding-insom-nia.html?iid=LHC_understandingInsomnia&utm_campaign=sem1h09&utm_medium=sem&utm_source=googleppc&utm_content=insomnia-d&utm_term=insomnia&cid=sem1h09ggle_insomnia

Chapter 1 – God's Rest Promised

4.   Thayer and Smith. Greek lexicon entry for Parakletos. The New Testament Greek Lexicon. www.studylight.org/lex/grk/view.cgi?number=3875
5.   Webster's II New Riverside University Dictionary. Boston: The Riverside Publishing Company, 1984

Chapter 2 – Flowing With Milk and Honey

6.   www.ohr.edu/ask_db/ask_main.php/234/Q5/
7.   Poverty, WordNet ® 2.0, © 2003 Princeton University
8.   Prosperity, American Heritage® Dictionary of the English Language, Fourth Edition, Copyright © 2000 by Houghton Mifflin Company. Published by Houghton Mifflin Company
9.   Chapter 3, p. 32, Randy Alcorn, Money, Possessions and Eternity, Tyndale House Publishers, Inc.

Chapter 3 – An Open Heaven

10.   Jamieson, Robert, D.D. "Commentary on Isaiah 55." Commentary Critical and Explanatory on the Whole Bible. www.studylight.org/com/jfb/view.cgi?book=isa&chapter=055. 1871.
11.   Easton, Matthew George. Entry for "Fir." Easton's Bible Dictionary. www.studylight.org/dic/ebd/view/cgi?number=T1333
12.   Gill, John. "Commentary on Isaiah 55:13." The New John Gill Exposition of the Entire Bible. www.studylight.org/com/geb/view.cgi?book=isa&chapter=055&verse=013. 1999.

Chapter 4 – Thank God for Your Wilderness

13.   www.middletownbiblechurch.org/crisesod/crises5.htm

Chapter 7 – He Will Exalt You

14.   Page 547, Illustrated Dictionary of the Bible, Herbert Lockyer, Sr. with F.F. Bruce and R.K. Harrison, copyright 1986, by Thomas Nelson Publishers, Nashville, Tennessee.

Chapter 8 – Shalom – Living In God's Rest

15.   www.emetministries.com/TheJoyofShalom.htm
16.   www.myredeemerlives.com/biblestudies/namesofgodstudy.html#nissi-shalom. Posted March 28, 2006.

Chapter 9 – If You Come, You Can Rest

17.   pp. 162-163. Intercessory Prayer, Pastor Dutch Sheets, Regal Books, 1957 Eastman Avenue, Ventura, California 93003, copyright 1997.
18.   Smith, William, Dr. Entry for "Raven." Smith's Bible Dictionary. www.studylight.org/dic/sbd/view.cgi?number=T3599. 1901.
19.   p. 143. Harold Best, Music through the Eyes of Faith, Harper Collins Publishers, 10 East 53rd Street, New York, New York 10022, copyright 1993

20.   p.26. Warren Wiersbe, Real Worship, Baker Books, 6030 East Fulton Road, Ada, Michigan 49301, copyright 2000

General Index

About the Author

Antonio Palmer began preaching at the age of 23. He has spent more than 10 years as the senior pastor of The Burning Bush Ministries in Annapolis, Maryland. He has extensive experience in evangelism, missions, and outreach, traveling throughout the United States and in other countries such as Mexico, Israel and Kenya. He preaches and teaches with authority and revelation and is often a keynote speaker at various conferences and revivals. He is the director of The Ark National and Global Outreach (TANGO) and vice presiding bishop of The Ark, Inc. Bishop Palmer and his wife Barbara resides in Maryland and they are blessed to be the parents of their radical-for-Jesus son, Randy.

To schedule Bishop Palmer as a guest speaker for your event, please contact him at:

antonio.palmer@ymail.com.

Kingdom Kaught Publishing, LLC |1242 Painted Fern Rd Denton MD 21629 |
www.kingdomkaughtpublishing.com

Printed in the United States
221574BV00001B/1/P

9 780982 455005